HOCKEY

HOCKEY

Subhash K. Goyal

CRESCENT
PUBLISHING CORPORATION

[The responsibility for the facts stated, conclusions reached and plagiarism, if any, in this book is entirely that of the Author. And the Publisher bears no responsibility for them, whatsoever.]

Hockey

First Published : 2009

ISBN 978-81-8342-154-6

Published by :

CRESCENT PUBLISHING CORPORATION
4831/24, Prahlad Street,
Ansari Road, Darya Ganj,
New Delhi - 110002
Ph. : 23272541, 23257835
Fax : 91- 011- 23257835
e-mail : campusbooks@hotmail.com

Printed at :
Roshan Offset Printers
Delhi

Preface

The national sport of India, hockey a stick and ball game related to cricket, ice hockey and lacrosse, originated in ancient 'Persia and Greece and assumed its current form after it spread to Europe. The English organised the game, which they called *hockie* and the French called hoquet, and instituted most of the modern rules. Because of its extreme popularity in British colonies, particularly in India, England and its former possession have dominated hockey on an international platform.

This book in the series of books on sports concentrates its focus on the game of hockey. It engages in a comprehensive discussion of the history of the game, moving on the detail the rules of hockey, its equipment, its organised tournaments, its sporting stars and the defining moments of the game. In addition, it also present forth an articulate and incisive presentation of the contemporary status of hockey, dealing with its issues and problems as well.

It is hoped that this up-to-date and comprehensive text on hockey is enjoyed by all hockey enthusiasts.

Subhash K. Goyal

Contents

1

Introduction to Hockey

Hockey is any of a family of sports in which two teams compete by trying to maneuver a ball, or a hard, round disc called a puck, into the opponent's net or goal, using a hockey stick. The dominant version of hockey in a particular region tends to be known simply as hockey, other forms being more fully qualified.

Field Hockey

Field hockey is played on gravel, natural grass, sand-based or water-based artificial turfs, with a small, hard ball. The game is popular among both males and females in many countries of the world, particularly in Europe, India, Pakistan, Australia, New Zealand, South Africa and South Asia. In most countries, the game is played between single-sex sides, although it can be played by mixed-sex sides. In the United States and Canada it is played predominantly by women.

The 116-member governing body is the International Hockey Federation (FIH). Field Hockey has been played at each summer Olympic Games since 1908. Modern field hockey sticks are J-shaped and constructed of a composite of wood, glass fibre or carbon fibre (sometimes both) and have a curved hook at the playing end, a flat surface on the playing side and curved surface on the rear side.

There are 4000-year-old drawings in Egypt of a game resembling field hockey being played. While modern field hockey appeared in the mid-18th century in England, primarily in schools, it was not until the first half of the 19th century that it became firmly established. The first club was created in 1849 at Blackheath in south-east London.

Ice Hockey

Ice hockey is played on a large flat area of ice, using a three inch (76.2 mm) diameter vulcanised rubber disc called a puck. This puck is often frozen before high-level games to decrease the amount of bouncing and friction on the ice. The game is contested between two teams of skaters. The game is played all over North America, Europe and in many other countries around the world to varying extent.

The 64-member governing body is the International Ice Hockey Federation, (IIHF). Men's ice hockey has been played at the Winter Olympics since 1924, and was in the 1920 Summer Olympics. Women's ice hockey was added to the Winter Olympics in 1998. North America's National Hockey League (NHL) is the strongest professional ice hockey league, drawing top ice hockey players from around the globe. The NHL rules are slightly different from those used in Olympic ice hockey—the periods are 20 minutes long, counting downwards. There are three periods. In some situations, the puck is frozen prior to the start of a game to limit bouncing.

Ice hockey sticks are long L-shaped sticks made of wood, graphite, or composites with a blade at the bottom that can lie flat on the playing surface when the stick is held upright and can curve either way as to help a left- or right-handed player gain an advantage. Variations in curves include its lie and its curve type. Most companies that produce sticks have sponsored players and in return, use their custom curve on publicly retailed sticks. To shoot with a left curved stick, the stick is held with the right hand at the top and the left hand partway down the shaft. To shoot with a right curved stick, the stick is held with the left hand at the top and the right hand partway down the shaft. Most people who are right handed shoot with a left curved stick, and most people who are left handed shoot with a right curved stick. This keeps their dominant hand at the top of the stick, allowing more control. Sticks also have flex numbers, a number on the stick that can go from zero to 100. It indicates how much the stick will bend before breaking when pressed on the ice. This flexing is what enables slapshots.

There are early representations and reports of hockey-type games being played on ice in the Netherlands, and reports from Canada from the beginning of the nineteenth century, but the modern game was initially organised by students at McGill University, Montreal in 1875 who, by two years later, codified the first set of ice hockey rules and organised the first teams.

Street Hockey

Another form of popular hockey is street hockey.

Roller Hockey

Inline hockey is a variation of roller hockey very similar to ice hockey, from which it is derived. Inline hockey is played by two teams, consisting of four skaters and one goalie, on a dry rink divided into two halves by a center line, with one net at each end of the rink. The game is played in four 15-minute periods with a variation of the ice hockey off-side rule. Icings are also called, but are usually referred to as illegal clearing. For rink dimensions and an overview of the rules of the game, see IIHF Inline Rules (official rules). Some leagues and competitions do not follow the IIHF regulations, in particular USA Inline and Canada Inline.

Roller Hockey (Quad)

Roller hockey (Quad) Roller Hockey is the overarching name for a roller sport that has existed long before inline skates were invented. Roller hockey has been played in sixty countries worldwide and so has many names worldwide. Sometimes the sport is called Quad Hockey, Hóquei em Patins, International Style Ball hockey, Rink hockey and Hardball hockey depending on the part of the world it is played. Roller Hockey was a demonstration rollersport in the 1992 Barcelona summer Olympics.

Unicycle Hockey

Unicycle hockey is similar to roller or inline hockey, however, each player must be mounted on their unicycle (with both feet on the pedals) to play at the ball. The ball is similar weight and bounce to a "dead" tennis ball and sticks are identical to roller hockey sticks. Each team consists of four players and one goalie, and substitution is allowed at any point in the game. Two common penalties are SUB (Stick Under Bike) and SIB (Stick In Bike) and result in a free shot being awarded to the player that was fouled upon. Players must also keep one hand on the end of the stick at all times and never allow the head of the stick to be lifted above waist height.

Other Forms of Hockey

Other games derived from hockey or its predecessors include the following:

— Ball hockey is played in a gym using sticks and a ball, often a tennis ball with the fuzz removed.

— Air hockey is played indoors with a puck on an air-cushion table.

— Bandy is played with a ball on a football-sized ice arena, typically outdoors. It is in some ways field hockey played on ice, but bandy has in fact more in common with association football (soccer).

— Beach Hockey was a professional league that played for three seasons at Huntington Beach, California. The game was played on inline skates at a rink. The league was canceled after ESPN stopped funding them due to low ratings.

— Broomball is played on an ice hockey rink, but with a ball instead of a puck and a "broom" (actually a stick with a small plastic implement on the end) in place of the ice hockey stick. Instead of using skates, special shoes are used that have very soft rubbery soles to maximize grip while running around.

— Bubble hockey is played in a plastic sealed table with the 'players' being moved by the use of pushing and turning rods.

— Floorball, or floor hockey, is a form of hockey played in a gymnasium or in sport halls.using a plastic puck or hollow ball, and plastic sticks.

— Foot hockey is played using a bald tennis ball or rolled up pair of socks and using only the feet. It is popular at elementary schools in the winter.

— Gym hockey is a form of ice hockey played in a gymnasium. It uses sticks with foam ends and a foam ball or a plastic puck.

— Hurling and Camogie are Irish games bearing some resemblance to—and notable differences from—hockey.

— Indoor field hockey is an indoor variation of field hockey.

— Mini hockey (Popularly known as "Mini-Sticks") is a form of hockey which is played in basements of houses. Players get down on their knees, using a miniature plastic stick, usually about 15 inches (38 cm) long and a small blue ball or a soft, fabric covered mini puck. They shoot into miniature goals as well. This is popular throughout North America, though it has not yet made the jump to Europe. In England this refers to a seven-a-side version of Field Hockey, played on an area equivalent to half a normal pitch for younger players, see Minkey (Mini Hockey)

— Polo is a form of hockey played mounted on horseback.

— PowerHockey is a form of hockey for persons requiring the use of an electric (power) wheelchair in daily life. PowerHockey is a competitive sports opportunity for the physically disabled.

— Ringette is an ice hockey variant that was designed for female players; it uses a straight stick and a rubber ring in place of a puck. Note: Ringette distances itself from hockey as it has its own set of rules and is closely related to a mix of lacrosse and basketball.

— Rinkball is a Scandinavian team sport, played in an ice hockey rink with a ball.

— Rossall Hockey is a variation played at Rossall School on the sea shore in the winter months. Its rules are a mix of field hockey, Rugby and the Eton Wall Game.

— Shinny is an informal version of ice hockey.

— Shinty is a Scottish Highlands game

— Skater hockey is a variant of inline hockey, played with a ball.

— Sledge hockey is a form of ice hockey played by the disabled. The players sit on sleds, and push themselves up and down the ice with picks on the butt end of their shortened hockey sticks. The game is played with many of the same rules as regular ice hockey.

— Spongee is a cross between ice hockey and broomball and is most popular in Manitoba, Canada. A stick and puck are used as in hockey (the puck is a softer version called a "sponge puck"), and the same soft-soled shoes used in broomball are worn. The rules are basically the same as ice hockey, but one variation has an extra player on the ice called a "rover".

— Table hockey is played indoors with a table-top game.

— Underwater hockey is played on the bottom of a swimming pool.

— Nok Hockey A table-top version of hockey played with no defense and a small block in front of the goal.

2

Field Hockey

Field hockey is a popular sport for men and women in many countries around the world. Its official name and the one by which it is usually known is hockey. However in some countries and in some encyclopedic references by way of distinguishing it from other sports with the same name it is formally known as Field hockey.

Hockey has several regular and prestigious international tournaments for both men and women. These events include the Olympic Games, the quadrennial Hockey World Cups, the annual Champions Trophies and World Cups for juniors. Indian and Pakistani national teams dominated men's hockey until the early 1980s, winning four of the first five world cups, but have become less prominent recently with The Netherlands, Germany, Australia and Spain gaining importance since the late 1980s. Other strong men's hockey playing nations include Argentina, England and South Korea.

The Netherlands was the predominant international women's team before hockey was added to Olympic events. In the early 1990s, Australia emerged as the strongest women's country although retirement of a number of key players has weakened the team. Other important women's teams are India, China, Korea, Argentina and Germany.

The International Hockey Federation (FIH) is the global governing body of the sport. It organises major international field hockey events such as the Hockey World Cup and Women's Hockey World Cup. The Hockey Rules Board under FIH is responsible for producing rules for the sport.

Many countries have extensive club competitions for both junior and senior players. Despite the large number of participants, club hockey is not a particularly large spectator sport and few players can afford to play professionally. In North America field hockey is widely regarded as a girls' and women's sport, especially as many schools and universities field teams. However, there are many men's and mixed leagues, especially in Canada. In Argentina, despite the strength of the men's national side, it is widely considered to be a women's sport.

In those countries where winter conditions prevent play outdoors field hockey is played indoors during the off-season. This indoor variant, known as indoor field hockey, differs from its outdoor parent in a number of respects. For example, it is 6-a-side rather than 11, the field of play is vastly reduced to approximately 40m x 20m; the shooting circles are 9m not 14.4m; players may not raise the ball outside the circle nor hit it. The sidelines are also replaced with barriers to rebound the ball off.

History of Field Hockey

Hockey-like games where teams attempt to place a ball or puck into their opponent's goal using sticks have been found throughout history and the world. Historical records show that game was played in various antique civilisations, although it is not possible to know exactly when and where the game began. 4,000-year-old drawings found in the Beni-Hasen tombs, in the Nile Valley, Egypt depicted men playing the sport. Other traces show that the Arabs, the Persians, the Romans (a version called paganica), the Ethiopians, as well as the Aztecs were playing their own variation of the game.

The first evidence of a team game was found on bases of statues that were part of the wall built by Themistocles in 478 B.C. Six men are carrying hooked sticks, two of which are opposing each other over a ball in what looks like the bully that starts modern games. The Irish game of hurling dates from at least 1272 B.C. European settlers in Argentina in the 16th century described a hockey-like game of the Araucano Indians called chueca (or 'the twisted one' from the twisted end of the stick used by players). In Western Australia, early white settlers witnessed Noongar people played a game called dumbung, in which bent sticks were used to hit a ball made of dried sap from the native peartree.

In the Middle Ages, hockey-like games were played throughout Europe, cambuca (or comocke or cammock; compare modern camogie) in England, shinty in Scotland, jeu de mail in France, and het kolven in The Netherlands. There are various depictions in cathedral windows (Canterbury and Gloucester), a book (Decretal of Gysors), and other artefacts. Clubbes, hurl-bat, shinnops, jowling, baddins, and doddorts were all games played in different parts of England. Both Edward III and Richard II tried to ban cambuca and bandy-ball as an interference with archery practice.

The origin of the word hockey is obscure. Hockie was forbidden in the Statutes of Galway in 1527. The word may derive from comocke and the Anglo-Saxon word for 'hook', hok; alternatively, it may come from the French word for a shepherd's crook, hocquet.

Modern Hockey

A game called hockey was being played in English public schools in the early 19th century. Lord Lytton wrote in 1853 that On the common some young men were playing at hockey. That old-fashioned game, now very uncommon in England, except at schools.... Hockey's popularity increased with that of other team games. The first club was Blackheath, perhaps formed in 1849 in southeast London (though there are reports of players from before 1840). The game played there was rougher than the modern version, played on a very large field (247m by 64m), and used a cube of black rubber and rough sticks planed on one side.

The modern game was developed on the other side of London by Middlesex cricket clubs, especially Teddington. The members of these clubs were looking for winter exercise, but did not particularly care for football. In 1871, members of the Teddington cricket club, who had recently moved to play in Bushy Park, were looking for a winter activity. They experimented with a 'stick' game, based loosely on the rules of association football. Teddington played the game on the smooth outfield of their cricket pitch and used a cricket ball, so allowing smooth and predictable motion. By 1874 they had begun to draw up rules for their game, including banning the raising of the stick above shoulder height and stipulating that a shot at goal must take place within the circle in front of it.

An association was formed in 1875, which dissolved after seven years, but in 1886 the Hockey Association was formed by seven London clubs and representatives from Trinity College, Cambridge. Blackheath were one of the founder members, but refused to accept the rules drawn up by the other clubs and left to found the National Hockey Union. The Union failed, but the Association grew rapidly.

They rejected a form of the game that involved a 7oz (200g) rubber cube, catching, marking and scrimmaging, based on rugby football, at the time favoured by the Blackheath club. The Teddington club chose to limit the number per side to eleven, and preferred to play with old cricket balls. They also introduced the idea of the striking circle ('the dee' or 'D'), and they played several games in Bushy Park, in the winter of 1871. Clubs were also set up in Richmond and Surbiton in 1874, and inter-club matches were played between them and Teddington. The game grew sporadically, as the clubs didn't always agree on the rules!

In the late 19th century, largely due to the British army, the game spread throughout the British Empire, leading to the first international competition in 1895 (Ireland 3, Wales 0). The International Rules Board was founded in 1895, and hockey first appeared at the Olympic Games as a men's competition at 1908 Olympic Games in London, with only three teams: England, Ireland and Scotland. Men's hockey became a permanent fixture at the Olympics at the 1928 Olympic Games, at Amsterdam.

The first step towards an international structuring occurred in 1909, when England and Belgium agreed to recognise each other for international competitions, soon joined in by the French federation. In 1924, the International Hockey Federation (FIH, Fédération Internationale de Hockey) was founded in Paris, under the initiative of the French man, Paul Léautey, as a response to hockey's omission from the 1924 Paris Game. The founding members were Austria, Belgium, Czechoslovakia, France, Hungary, Spain, and Switzerland. The development of the FIH owes a lot to the work of Réné George Frank, a Belgium, in the years after the Second World War until the 1970's. Men's hockey united under the FIH in 1970, when the Hockey

Association joined and the International Rules Board became part of the FIH's structure.

The game had been taken to India by British servicemen, and the first clubs formed there in Calcutta in 1885. The Beighton Cup and the Aga Khan tournament had commenced within ten years. Entering the Olympic Games in 1928, India won all five of its games without conceding a goal, and went on to win in 1932 until 1956, and then in 1964 and 1980. Pakistan won in 1960, 1968, and 1984.

The International Hockey Federation has continued to grow and now consists of 112 member associations, spread around five continents.

Ladies Hockey

Women's hockey developed separately from men's hockey. Women do not seem to have played hockey widely before the modern era. Women's hockey was first played at British Universities and schools, and the first club, Molesey Ladies Hockey Club, was founded in 1887. The first national association was the Irish Ladies Hockey Union in 1894, and though rebuffed by the Hockey Association, women's hockey grew rapidly around the world. This led to the formation of the International Federation of Women's Hockey Associations (IFWHA) in 1927, though this did not include initially many continental European countries where women played as sections of men's associations and were affiliated to the FIH. The IFWHA held conferences every three years, and the tournaments associated with these were the primary IFWHA competitions. These tournaments were non-competitive until 1975.

By the early 1970's there were 22 associations with women's sections in the FIH and 36 associations in the IFWHA. Discussions were started about a common rule book. The FIH introduced competitive tournaments in 1974, forcing the acceptance of the principle of competitive hockey by the IFWHA in 1973. It took until 1982 for the two bodies to merge, but this allowed the introduction of women's hockey to the Olympic games from 1980 where, as in the men's game, The Netherlands, Germany, and Australia have been consistently strong.

Synthetic Revolution

In the early 1970s, the "synthetic grass" fields began to be used for hockey, with the first Olympic Games on this surface being held at the 1976 Montreal edition.

Synthetic pitches are now mandatory for all the international tournaments and for most of the national competitions. While hockey is still played on grass fields at some local levels and lesser national divisions, it has been replaced by astroturf almost everywhere in the western world.

The game, as well as the material used to play it, has taken a definitive turn with the introduction of the synthetic field, gaining in speed, losing, some would say, in skills. What is clear is that the game has deeply evolved. In order to take into account the specificities of this surface, new tactics, new techniques (such as the indian dribble) have been developed and new rules have been settled, often, in order to frame, these new techniques. Regarding the evolution of the hockey player material, the sticks have changed shape, with the bent head at the bottom, which used to be about 15 centimetres long, becoming much stubbier. The extra length was no longer necessary, as the ball travelled much straighter on the flatter synthetic fields.

The shorter length made playing the ball with the "backhand" (playing with the head of the stick to the player's left, with the head rotated 180 degrees from its usual position) much easier, increasing the speed with which this tactic, often used for evasive manoeuvres, could be used. It also makes trapping the ball by placing the entire stick on the ground, with the point of the head resting on the ground to the player's left, possible, and this stopping technique is now universal for trapping the ball at penalty corners. The sticks also tend to become more and more stiff as to hit the ball harder. Fibreglass, carbon fibre and kevlar were first applied to the traditional wood core in early 1970s. Sticks with an aluminium core have been produced but are now prohibited due to the danger they pose when broken. Wooden sticks are less and less common, and players are now playing with sticks entirely made of synthetic composite materials.

The goalkeeper equipment has followed the same trend, becoming more and more able to resist to strength of the balls hit by these new generation sticks. Helmets have become compulsory, padding is thicker and of more shock-absorbing (and reflecting) foam material, and more areas of the body are padded. The new equipment is very expensive and is often a considerable burden for clubs or individual goalkeepers to purchase. The composition of the hockey ball has also changed, from a leather ball with a seam similar to a cricket ball, to a seamless, usually dimpled hard plastic ball. These plastic balls are cheaper, more durable, more consistent in their behaviour, and are unaffected by water; a key requirement in water-moderated synthetic fields used in elite-level hockey.

Ancillary player equipment has also changed. The studded boots for grass fields are banned (and were in any case very uncomfortable) on synthetics, and have been replaced with boots specifically designed for synthetic turf. Shin guards have improved padding. Many players have taken to wearing padded gloves, particularly on their left hand, both to protect against contact and allow them to scrape that hand (while holding the stick) across the synthetic turf without injury. Finally, the wearing of mouth guards to protect the teeth is now compulsory for safety in many countries.

Rules Evolution

The rules of the game have widely changed. The main issues have been

— to adapt the game to the new synthetic fields introduced in 1980's.

— to enhance comprehension from non-players in order to gain TV coverage Some of these rules changes:

— the FIH eliminated the offside rule (similar to offside in football) in the mid-1990's in order to increase scoring opportunities.

— Constant modifications of the penalty corner rules in order to minimize its importance in the game and its readability

— limitation of the bow of sticks in order to limit the increasing use and power of drag flicks

Field of Play

Most hockey field dimensions were originally fixed using whole numbers of imperial measures and are expressed as such in this article. It is, nevertheless, the metric measurements shown in parenthesis which are the current official dimensions of the field of play as laid down by the International Hockey Federation (FIH) in the "Rules of Hockey 2007".

The game is played between two teams of eleven players on a 100 × 60 yard (91.4 m × 55 m) rectangular field. At each end there is a goal 7 feet (2.14 m) high and 12 feet (3.66 m) wide, and a semi-circle 16 yards (14.63 m)

from the goal known as the shooting circle (or D or arc), with a dotted line 5 yards (5 m) from the semi-circle, as well as lines across the field 25 yards (22.9 m) from each end-line and in the center of the field. A spot, called the penalty spot or stroke mark, is placed 7 yards (6.4 m) from the center of each goal.

Traditional grass pitches are far less common in modern hockey with most hockey being played on synthetic surfaces. Since the 1970's sand based pitches were favoured as they dramatically speed up the pace of the game. However, in recent years there has been a massive increase in the number of 'water based' artificial turfs. Water based astro turfs enable the ball to be transferred more quickly than on the original sand based surfaces and it is this characteristic that has made them the surface of choice for international and national league competitions. Water based surfaces are also less abrasive than the sand based variety and hence reduce the level of injury to players when they come into contact with the surface. The FIH are now proposing that new surfaces being laid should be of a hybrid variety which require less watering. This is due to the negative ecological effects of the high water requirements of water based astros.

Rules and Play

Players are permitted to play the ball with any part of the stick other than the rounded side (back). The flat side is always on the "natural" side for a right-handed person—there are no "left-handed" hockey sticks (for actual use in play, some have been made as novelties).

Teams consist of eleven players on the field, and up to five substitutes. Substitutions are not limited but may not be made during a penalty corner. There are no set positions (even a goalkeeper is not required under the

2007 rules), but most teams arrange themselves (in a similar way to football (soccer) teams) into fullbacks (defence), midfielders (halfback) and forwards (front line)). Many teams include a single sweeper. The rules do not specify a minimum number of players for a match to take place, but most competitions have some local ruling on this, with seven players being a common minimum.

One player from each team may be designated the goalkeeper. Goalkeepers must wear a suitable helmet with full face mask and are also permitted to wear protective padding, including large leg guards, kickers and gloves. Although goalkeepers may block or deflect the ball with any part of their bodies, and propel the ball with their feet (and from 2007 any other part of their equipment in a "goal-saving action"), they must always carry a stick, and normal stick rules apply. Goalkeepers are permitted to play the ball outside their defensive circle (scoring area or "D"), but must only use the stick in this circumstance. Fully protected goalkeepers are prohibited from passing their side's defensive 23m line during play, unless they are taking a penalty stroke.

General play

For the purposes of the rules, all players on the team in possession of the ball are attackers, and those on the team without the ball are defenders. The match is officiated by two field umpires. Traditionally each umpire generally controls half of the field, divided roughly diagonally. These umpires are often assisted by a technical bench including a timekeeper and record keeper.

Prior to the start of the game, a coin is tossed and the winning captain can choose a starting end or start with the ball. The game time is divided into two equal halves of 35 minutes each, with five minutes for half-time. At the start of each half, as well as after goals are scored, play is started with a pass from the centre of the field. All players must start in their defensive half, but the ball may be played in any direction along the floor. Each team starts with the ball in one half, and the team that conceded the goal has possession for the restart.

Field players may only play the ball with the face of the stick. Tackling is permitted as long as the tackler does not make contact with the attacker or his stick before playing the ball (contact after the tackle may also be penalised if the tackle was made from a position where contact was inevitable). Further, the player with the ball may not deliberately use his body to push a defender out of the way.

Field players may not play the ball with their feet, but if the ball accidentally hits the feet, and the player gains no benefit from the contact, then the contact is not penalised. Although there has been a change in the wording of this rule from 1 January 2007, the current FIH umpires' briefing instructs umpires not to change the way they interpret this rule.

Obstruction typically occurs in three circumstances—when a defender comes between the player with possession and the ball without first performing a legitimate tackle; when a defender's stick comes between the attacker's stick and the ball or makes contact with the attacker's stick; and also when (usually deliberately) blocking the opposition's passage to the ball.

When the ball passes over the sidelines, it is returned to play with a sideline hit, taken by a member of the team whose players were not the last to touch the ball before crossing the sideline. If it crosses the backline after last touched by an attacker, a 15 m hit. A 15 m hit is also awarded for offenses committed by the attacking side within 15 m of the end of the pitch they are attacking.

Set Plays

Free hits are awarded when offences are committed outside the scoring circles. The ball may be hit or pushed once in any direction by the team offended against. However, the ball must not be judged to be intentionally raised by the umpire from a free hit, or the umpire can "reverse" the decision. This means that the team who were defending are now attacking, and can lead to swift counter attacks. Opponents must move 5 m from the ball when a free hit is awarded, and for attacking free hits within 5 m of the circle all attackers other than the one taking the hit must also be 5 m away.

As mentioned above, a 15 m hit is awarded if an attacking player commits a foul forward of that line, or if the ball passes over the backline off an attacker. These hits are taken in line with where the foul was committed (taking a line parallel with the sideline between where the offence was committed, or the ball went out of play). If the attack commit a foul in the circle they are attacking, the defence additionally has the option to take the free hit anywhere in that circle.

A long corner is awarded if the ball goes over the backline after last being touched by a defender. Long corners are played by the attacking team and involve a free hit on the sideline 5 m from the corner of the field closest to where the ball went out of play. In some areas these are also known as long hits.

The short or penalty corner is a rather complicated set play that is awarded against a defending team when they commit any offence their defensive circle (that is not penalised by a Penalty Stroke), and may be awarded when a deliberate offence is committed in the defending 23 m area, or when the defending team deliberately plays the ball over the back line.

Short corners begin with five defenders (including the keeper) arranged along the backline. All other defenders must return to the centre line until the ball is in play. Attacking players begin the play standing outside the scoring circle, except for one attacker who starts the corner by playing the ball from a mark 10 m either side of the goal (the circle has a 14.63 m radius). This player puts the ball into play by pushing or hitting the ball to the other attackers outside the circle; the ball must pass outside the circle before the attackers attempt to get a shot or deflection into the goal.

For safety reasons, the first shot of a penalty corner must not exceed 460mm high (the height of the "backboard" of the goal) at the point it crosses the goal line if it is hit. However, if the ball is deemed to below backboard height, the ball can be subsequently deflected above this height by another player (defender or attacker), providing that this deflection does not lead to danger. Note that the "Slap Hit" or "Slap" (a hitting motion, where the stick is kept on or close to the ground when hitting the ball) is classed as a hit for short corners, and so the first shot at goal must be below backboard height for this type of shot also.

If the first shot at goal in a short corner situation is a push, flick or scoop, in particular the drag flick (which has become popular at international and national league standards), the shot is permitted to rise above the height of the backboard, as long as the shot is not deemed dangerous to the defenders on the line. This form of shooting is becoming more and more popular as international level players are able to get nearly as much power through the drag-flick as a full blown hit on goal.

Penalty stroke

A penalty stroke (often referred to as a PS, a flick, or just as a stroke) is awarded when defenders commit a deliberate foul in the circle which deprives an attacker of possession or the opportunity to play the ball, when any breach prevents a probable goal, or if defenders repeatedly "break" or start to run from the backline before a penalty corner has started. This penalty pits a single attacker against the goalkeeper, and is taken from a spot 6.4 m out and directly in front of the goal. The goalkeeper must stand with heels on the goal line, and cannot move his feet until the ball is played, whilst the striker must start behind the ball and within playing distance of it (in other words he must be able to touch the ball with his stick). On the umpire's whistle, the striker may push or flick the ball at the goal, which the goalkeeper attempts to save.

The attacker is not permitted to take more than one shot, to fake or dummy the shot, or to move towards or interfere with the goalkeeper once the shot is taken. Hitting or dragging the ball is also forbidden. If the shot is saved, play is restarted with a 15 m hit to the defenders; if a goal is scored, play is restarted in the normal way. If the goalkeeper commits a foul which prevents a goal being scored, a penalty goal may be awarded, for other fouls by defenders, the result is normally that the stroke is retaken. If the taker commits a foul, it is treated as if the stroke has been saved, and play recommences with a 15 m hit. If another attacker commits a foul, then if a goal is scored it is voided, and the stroke retaken.

Dangerous Play

If the ball is raised off the ground in a manner that is, in the umpire's opinion, dangerous, the ball is turned over to the other team and they receive a free hit. The free hit is taken where the action that caused the danger occurred (that is, not where the danger itself occurs). The definition of a "dangerous ball" is a matter of interpretation by the umpires. Guidance in the rules states "a ball is considered dangerous when it causes legitimate evasive action by players"—but it also depends on the speed of the ball, the height to which it is raised, and the number of players near its path.

It is, however, legal to raise the ball to make an aerial pass, provided that the ball is both raised safely and brought down safely. The ball may only be lifted if the opposition players are further than 5m from the player raising the ball, and the ball is safely lifted above the players. Balls raised safely, but towards players of either side are deemed dangerous. When receiving an aerial ball, the initial receiver must be given 5m to bring down the ball safely, before they can be challenged by an opposition player. If there are two or more players attempting to receive the ball (usually from opposite teams), and it is not clear which player was first to be in position to receive the ball, then a free hit is given to the defending team (the team that did not raise the ball).

It is, however, legal to raise the ball when making a shot on goal (by hitting, flicking or scooping), but the shot must not be dangerous to any other players (for example, hitting the ball in the air towards goal with only the goalkeeper in the goal is safe-as the goalkeeper has protective padding, whereas hitting the ball in the air towards goal when there are a number of players between the striker and the goal can be classed as dangerous play). In general the ball may only deliberately be raised using a hit if the player is shooting at the goal.

It is not dangerous to lift the ball over an opponent's stick (or body), provided that the opponent is not required to take evasive action. For example, a skillful attacker may lift the ball over a defenders stick and run past them, however if the attacker lifts the ball into/at the defender's body, this would be classed dangerous.

Dangerous play rules also apply with relation to the usage of the stick. Players may not attempt to play at the ball above their shoulders (unless saving a goal). It will generally be considered dangerous play to hit the ball while it is in the air; the ball must be controlled first in this circumstance.

Warnings

Hockey uses a three-tier card system of warnings and suspensions:

— A Green card is a warning.

— A Yellow card is a temporary suspension, just like in rugby football, normally for a minimum of 5 minutes duration without substitution.

— A Red card, just like in association football, is a permanent exclusion from the rest of the game, without substitution, and in many circumstances will also result in the player being banned for a certain period of time or number of matches (this is governed by local playing conditions, rather than the rules of hockey).

Unlike football, a player may receive more than one green or yellow card. However they cannot receive the same card for the same offence (example two yellows for dangerous play), and the second must always be a more serious card. In the case of a second yellow card for a different breach of the rules, the temporary suspension would be expected to be of considerably longer duration than the first. However, local playing conditions may mandate that cards are awarded only progressively, and not allow any second awards.

Umpires may also advance a free-hit by up to 10m for dissent or other misconduct after a penalty has been awarded; or, if the free-hit would have been in the attacking 23m area, upgrade the penalty to a penalty corner.

The teams' object is to play the ball into their attacking circle and, from there, hit, push or flick the ball into the goal, scoring a point. The team with more goals after two 35-minute halves wins the game. The playing time may be shortened, particularly when younger players are involved, or for some tournament play.

Conditions for breaking ties are not laid down in the rules of hockey, but many associations will follow the procedure laid down in FIH tournament regulations which mandate 7.5 minutes each way of "golden goal" or "sudden death" extra time (i.e. the game ends as soon as one team scores). If scores are still level, then the game will be decided with penalty strokes, in much the same way that association football penalty shoot outs are conducted.

Other competitions may use alternative means of breaking a tie, for example, an extended period of golden goal extra time with a progressive reduction in the number of players each team can have on the field (usually termed "drop-offs"); if no goal is scored at the end of such extra time periods, again a result would be achieved using penalty strokes.

There are sometimes minor variations in rules from competition to competition; for instance, the duration of matches is often varied for junior competitions, or for carnivals. Different national associations also have slightly differing rules on player equipment.

In the United States, NCAA have their own rules for inter-collegiate competitions, and high school associations similarly play to different rules. This article assumes FIH rules unless otherwise stated. USA Field Hockey produces an annual summary of the differences.

Equipment

In Field hockey, each player carries a stick and cannot take part in the game without it. The stick is usually between 36″ and 38″ long and traditionally made of wood but now almost all sticks are 'composite'—made of a number of materials. They usually contain a combination of fibreglass, kevlar (or aramid) and carbon fibre composites. The more expensive a hockey stick the higher the proportion of carbon fibre it will have in it, up to around 80%.

Rules

Although the exact origin of field hockey remains unknown, historians have recorded a number of 4,000-year-old drawings found in the tomb at Beni-Hasen in the Nile Valley (Egypt) which showed men playing the sport. Throughout the following centuries, variations of the game were played by a spectrum of cultures ranging from Greeks and Romans to Ethiopians, Indians and Aztecs. In most of these cultures a single wooden stick with a curved end, probably a sapling or a suitable tree branch, immediately available, was used rather than a purpose 'manufactured' sports item.

Finally after centuries of different variations of hockey, (including a version in England, sometime prior to 1860, in which. because of the very hilly heathland area in which it was played, a rubber cube and not a ball was used,) the game became more organised and regularised.

By 1886, when an association of clubs was formed and the game became more standardised,the modern game as we know it began (and a white painted cricket ball had become the standard object to play with). The game had also by this time divided into various branches which developed as separate sports. Shinty, a game popular in Scotland, uses both sides of a round stick with a curved end, which is shaped in a similar way to a walking stick; the Irish game, hurley, uses both sides of a stick which is flat on both sides and shaped somewhat like bill-hook with an axe-like handle. The stick in England, possibly because of the close association with it of cricket players, developed with a stick with just one flat playing side, the left face, below a round grip area—with the use of the right-face side, which is rounded prohibited—an oddity that had a profound effect on the later development of the hockey stick and of the game itself.

Initially there were only six Rule requirements applying to the hockey stick.

— The stick had to be flat on the playing side (the left side when the 'toe' of the stick-head is facing away from the user).

— It had to able to be passed completely through a two inch (internal diameter) ring.

— The stick was to be smooth (no rough or sharp edges).

— The head of the stick was to be a) curved and b) made from wood.

— A maximum and minimum weight were specified, 28oz and 12oz respectively.

Description

By Rule a hockey stick comprises two parts (even if all one piece) A 'Head' and a 'Handle'. Historically the stick was made in two separate parts and the Head was spliced to the Handle, in much the same way as the handle of a cricket bat is spliced to the blade.

Today many hockey sticks are manufactured from man-made materials (so called 'composite sticks') in moulds and in one operation, so do not have a separate joined head and handle. By Rule the 'head' part was from the bottom end of the splice with the stick-handle to the base of the curve of the stickhead and the handle was from the bottom of the splice with stickhead to the top of the stick (where it was gripped in play).

The need to inspect that a stick complied with new regulations, concerning materials used, and with new regulations, concerning the permitted shape of the 'head' and handle led to a change in the description of the 'head' and handle parts. This article will examine the transition from the shape of sticks in the era before the First World War to the Hockey World Cup in Willesden England in 1986 and from there, to the modern designs. Many of these changes have come about because of the availability of new materials and changes to playing surfaces but this article will be focused more on the reasons for stick shapes and the differences between them, rather than on an exploration of construction materials and reinforcements or 'artificial' playing surfaces.

Hockey stick head parts were commonly made from large timbers, 4¼" x 4¼" in section and more than 4' in length, which were bent in presses after steam treatment, dried and then cut into four 'bats' for later shaping with saw and adze.

This type of manufacture is still in use today, although significant numbers of stickheads are now of laminated timber manufacture and more and more hockey sticks are now being made entirely from 'composite' materials, in one piece, in moulds.

In the upper left corner of the picture of the press there is a small insert showing the kind of head bend these presses were originally designed to produce. That stick is circa 1962/3. Near the lower right of the picture and unfortunately, cut off, is a view of the typical 'horseshoe' shape bending produced by the machine. A heavy cast iron staple was hammered across the ends while (while the timber is still in the press) and the piece was further restrained by a flexible steel strap, then removed from the press and allowed to dry out and 'set' for a few days before cutting. This particular machine was modified to run from an electric motor, but it was originally hand operated and probably dates from a time before electricity was available (or reliable) in that part of Pakistan. The boss in the centre would also have been modified to produce the tighter head bends required at the time this photograph was taken.

The first major developments to what was later termed the 'English style' stick (and the method of play with such sticks) occurred in India. (The game in its modern form was apparently brought to India by the British Army, although there does not appear to be any specific evidence of this. But certainly hockey was played by the British forces in India). At that time the stickhead was very long (in excess of 12"—300mm) and made from an indigenous British timber, ash. The Indians then produced sticks with a much shorter head length and a tighter heel bend and used mulberry, which is tougher than ash, but has similar bending characteristics and weight and is easy to work. This development changed the nature of the game, led to the 'Indian dribble' and to Indian dominace of the game in the first half of the twentieth century.

A hockey stick is occasionally used in the vertical position shown, but manipulating the movement and the direction of the ball in a controlled way (dribbling) is carried out in what is termed a 'dribbling crouch', when the handle of the stick will usually be angled between 35° and 55°. Hitting or pushing the ball can be done with the stick at any angle between the vertical and horizontal and recent changes to the rules allow even the edges of the stick to be used to sweep or strike at the ball on the ground. The various designs will be initially looked at with the handle at an angle of 45° to compare how they differ in the carrying out of the 'Indian dribble' i.e. controlling the direction of the ball by rotating the stickhead over the top/front of the ball rather than (or as well as) around the back of the ball (the English style dribble).The multi-layered stickhead diagram gives an idea of the changes in head lengths and shapes that occurred over a period of thirty years or so. It is intended to conduct an examination of some of these various head shapes with regard to the way they affect playing style and the method of using a hockey stick.

The first questions are:- Why was the stick-head shortened, surely that reduced the stopping area of the head? The answer lies in the fact that by Rule only one side of the stickhead could be used (at that time the ball could not be played with the 'edges' of the head or handle but with the flat side -or face side- only).

Using extreme examples is useful as a means of demonstrating effects that occur in less extreme configurations but are much more difficult to spot and therefore to explain. The first observation is an easy one. Top left. If the stick head is rotated onto the reverse (lighter colour) the Toe is not going to disappear into the ground to enable the reverse side of the stick to be presented to the ball—a vertical adjustment is necessary. Secondly, (top right) if the handle of the stick is kept at exactly the same angle and rotated, a horizontal adjustment is necessary to bring the reversed head to a position where contact will be made with the ball.

The third figure (bottom left) shows these adjustments having been made (and a change to the angle of the handle because the position of the hand holding the stick at the top would be about the same as it is when gripping the stick in the forehand position), but the area of stickhead making contact with the ball is very small; so control may not be adequate. The fourth figure (bottom right) demonstrates that to get good contact with the ball on a larger area of the reversed head, it is necessary to move the handle much nearer to the vertical. This means the player must bring the ball in very close to the feet and come to a more upright dribbling position— this in turn impairs the ability to scan the pitch and keep the ball in peripheral vision at the same time—a considerable disadvantage when dribbling to evade opponents.

So, although the long head stick was an adequate shape for a dribbling style which was based on moving the ball forward from directly behind the ball; and changes of direction could be achieved by rotating the stick around the back of the ball and/or moving the feet to either side of the ball, it was not so easy to use the long stickhead to bring the ball across the feet and back again, particularly when it was placed wide to the left of the feet of the player.(This left side position was compounded in difficulty with a very severe interpretation of 'obstruction', which prohibited shielding of the ball from an opponent. The game was also, at the time, seen as 'right-sided' and positioning the body between the ball and a close or closing opponent, approaching from the right hand side, was not allowed.) Reversed stick hitting, pushing and flicking would be short range skills and difficult to do accurately, if at all, especially when moving at speed.

Gradually over many years stickheads were made shorter and the 'heel' was made to a tighter bend. This process continued until the 'one piece' head could not be made to a sharper bend without the timber splitting out on the base. As it was, attempts to have the grain follow entirely the same curve as the bend, as it should for maximum strength were abandoned by some producers and an upturn to the 'toe' was sometimes achieved by cutting across the wood-grain at the 'toe' end of the 'head' to achieve the desired shape. Some manufacturers resorted to gluing a separate piece of wood on top of the 'toe' or glued additional strips of timber to the inner edge of the handle above the head to get the effect of a tighter 'heel' bend.

Some players were cutting part of the toe off their sticks, to achieve a shorter head, and rounding the end off,(although on the older styles this did nothing to tighten the bend to the 'heel' and often just ruined the stick). Predictably, there were sticks produced for the 1986 World Cup with heads with a horizontal length of only 95mm. The International players to whom they were handed out, tried them and then returned them as unusable.

What was the difficulty? It was twofold: 1) The 'toe' was so short that it could not be rotated completely over the top circumference of the ball and 2) When the stickhead was played around the back of the ball it 'ran off', because there was insufficient 'run length' to the stickhead. If, for example, a player 'propped' the ball while moving in a dribbling crouch (putting the stickhead over the front of the ball), drew the ball back towards his feet and then took the stickhead around the back of the ball to bring it forward again, perhaps moving the ball off in another direction (a common movement), the margin for error was so small that the ball could easily slip off the stickhead.

The ultra-short stickhead was to some extent based on the idea that the new artificial surfaces would lead to a style of hockey based on stopping the ball with the handle of the stick near horizontal to the ground and that dribbling to elude opponents would be almost eliminated with near continuous passing of the ball. Although there was a development of 'system hockey' that overcame the stick/ball skill deficiencies of the Europeans compared with India and Pakistan at the time, it was not as fluid as the kind of one and two touch passing game common in soccer and that 'ideal' was (and still is) a long way off.

Heel Bend

It may be noted from the diagram that no matter how 'tight' the 'heel' bend, reversing the stickhead over the ball, with a 'traditional' style hockey stick 'head', always requires both a vertical and horizontal adjustment of the stickhead position. This is not anywhere near as difficult as it was with the very long head stick and this sort of adjustment will be almost sub-conscious in an experienced player. Note too, that when the shaft is held vertically, the ball is more securely stopped, when on the ground, to the 'toe' side of the shaft rather than in the middle of the shaft.

Novice players frequently assume that the centre of the ball will align with the centre of the shaft when stopping the ball in this way and as a result, the ball deflects off to the 'heel' side and usually into their feet. Because of the 'heel' slope on the stickhead the 'vertical shaft' stop is actually much easier to carry out securely (when the ball is on the ground) if the handle is held at least 10° off the vertical, with the top of the handle sloped to the player's left. When the ball in the air, a little off the ground, below knee height for example, is often easier to 'catch' the ball correctly if the handle is vertical.

Hook

In 1982 a Dutch inventor, Toon Coolen, patented a hockey stick with a 'hook' head. The hockey stick manufacturers Grays took the design up in 1983 and the first mass-produced hockey sticks, with laminated timber 'head' parts, were manufactured in Pakistan. This new design was possible because of the development of epoxy resin glues that did not require perfectly dry timber for bonding and curing to a strength that could cope with the immense stresses placed on a stickhead when a hockey ball is struck with it.

By 1993 the 'Hook' Patent, had been ruled (following a court case in Germany) to protect only hook shapes within 20° of the vaguely written "nearly 180°" (referring to the degree of upturn of the 'toe' in relation to the shaft of the stick in the Patent Description; the 'shaft' of the handle being described a being bent through "nearly 180°" to form the hook shape of the stickhead). That opened the way for the appearance of more 'J' shaped stickheads and the gradual 'morphing' of the 'midi' shape with the 'hook' shape.

In that year also a Patent Application, lodged in Pakistan in 1987 by Martin Conlon, for a kinked shaft hockey stick, with a set-back Head (which was also hook shaped, but not to "near 180°"), was granted after strong opposition in Pakistan. (Indian and GB Patents had been granted in 1988, although the same company had also opposed the GB Patent Application). Mr Conlon designed and imported to the UK the first 'J' head sticks in 1990 but, prior to the 1993 decision, other distributors and manufacturers had been very reluctant to order made or produce hook style sticks of any sort, because of uncertainty about the strength of the Patent that 'ring-fenced' the 'Hook' hockey stick.

Modern hook

In the mid-90's the 'hook' head style hockey stick was relaunched, this time by the former German U21 International player Thomas Keiller. Bright colours, bold graphics and painted heads were introduced. Manufacturers became much more aware of the 'look' of their products and hockey sticks sold, particularly to new players, as much on colour and 'fashion' as strength and usability.

Today, across many brands, there is a choice of angle of hook upturn, 45°, 60°, 75°. A style of stick that almost no-one in Europe wanted to use in 1987, is in 2006 used almost universally played with; it is difficult now to find a player who is not using a hook style hockey stick and many of them have never used the 'shortie' style at all—just as many of the players of today have never played hockey on a natural grass pitch—the development of artificial surfaces has also had a significant effect on the ways in which hockey sticks are used.

New names have been coined to describe the various hook shapes but there is much confusion and overlapping of names. 'Maxi' and 'Mega' are also terms for styles of hook shape but there is no common agreement about what these terms mean outside of each 'brand' name that employs them: what one brand terms a 'midi' another calls a 'hook' but, basically, there are three types of hook. The near symmetrical 'U', a 'tight' or 'closed' toe shape, between 60° and 75° and an 'open' shape between 45°-55°. Where the 'toe' is shorter the same toe angles are generally referred to as 'midi'

'midi' Head

The death knell of the ultra short head was sounded in 1986, due to the introduction of the 'midi' 'head' shape, produced with a laminating process; although of course many players continued to use 'one piece' short head sticks for many years after that date and many thousands more of them were manufactured. The reason for the continued use of the 'one piece' was that the 'midi' length was similar to that of the more popular 'one piece' stickheads that had been around for the previous ten or so years. Some 'one piece' constructions were still being produced on presses on which the central 'boss' had not been modified and the 'heel' bend was 'slower' than on that of the production of the more aware manufacturers, but the more 'go ahead' manufacturers were producing a 'one piece' that could compete well with the laminated 'midi'—at least as far as 'playing functionality' was concerned.

The biggest 'casualty' of the 'midi' was the patented 'Hook' produced by the same company. It had not 'taken off' in the UK culture of the short-head stick and for a number of years after the 'midi' was introduced the 'Hook' was seen as something of a novelty, even as an indoor stick or a stick exclusively for goalkeepers. In fact versions of it were produced specifically for goalkeepers, with a very extended toe (6"—150mm or more) and that development continued until some were made with the 'toe' extending nearly the length of the handle and the FIH 'stepped in' and ruled that the vertical 'toe' limit was in future to be 4"—(100mm).

The 'Hook' was 124mm, measured horizontally across face of the stickhead, when the handle was held vertically; the 'midi' was 113mm ; many 'one piece' heads between 110mm and 115mm, and the unusable 'ultra short' 94mm. A difference of only 30mm between the head length of a stick that was considered cumbersome to one that was considered too short to easily play with. There were still many players playing quite happily with a stick with a head length of 7" (175mm), but players buying new sticks were now conscious of quite subtle differences in stick 'feel' and performance due to length, shape and the distribution of 'head' weight—not just the total ounce weight and the 'swing weight or balance' of the stick—and for the first time, in the years after 1986, were being offered a wide range of hockey sticks from a greatly increased number of manufacturers, from which to choose what suited them. After the arrival of the laminations, some brands were offering as many as ten different shapes or styles of stickhead on the traditional shaft. The arrival of 'composites' would complicate the picture further.

In the early 1990s there were an astonishing number and variety of hockey sticks on offer compared with what had been available ten years earlier. By 1992, hockey stick reinforcement was a big issue and 'composites' had been accepted into an (extended) FIH 'experimental trial period'. There were also hockey sticks with metal handles and inserted ply-wood heads (made by the American company Eastons, better known for making baseball bats), as well as the wide range of 'one piece' head sticks still produced and an expanding range of laminated 'midi' and laminated 'shorties'. The metal handled sticks were later banned for 'safety reasons', in what was widely regarded as a 'political' move by the FIH.

Set-back stickheads

The big headed 'Hook' also suffered for a short time from the appearance at the 1986 World Cup of the first sticks with set-back heads. There wasn't a significant impact but it (and others) added to the general confusion, as apparently 'everyone and his dog' were presenting new ideas in head shape. (Metal handled and fully composite sticks had not yet made an appearance so at the time the 'battle' was about head shape and length rather than materials and to a lesser extent, because hockey players at the time tended to be more 'traditionalist', the head/ handle configuration. Even reinforcement with fiberglass and carbon fibre was not the issue it was later to become.

One hockey stick produced by AREC for the French inventor, Jean Capét, had the centre of the handle aligned with the centre of the horizontal length of the head. There was a lot of promotion based on 'rotational balance' and the 'sweet spot' and 'power hitting'. The 'Hook' certainly felt out of rotational balance, especially to those who had been playing with short-head sticks that had been made with a very thin 'toe', so as to concentrate the weight of the head closer to the shaft.

Recurve Heads

The traditional small arc to the heel edge of the hockey stick had the effect of setting the stick-head back slightly. This aspect of stick design (of which the AREC hockey stick was an extreme example) was first explored just prior to the Men's Hockey World Cup of 1986 and resulted in the production of hockey sticks with a stick-head considerably more set-back in relation to the handle. The original design, aligning the centre line of the handle with the centre of the ball, in the common striking position, featured a counterbalancing 'kink' or protrusion to the handle on the 'toe' edge of the handle, just above the head of the stick. This invention of the 'kinked-shaft' and set-back head stick led directly to rules governing the amount of bend or 'permitted deviation' to the 'edge sides' of the hockey stick handle. Some of these were later termed 'recurve' heads (a description given to a later style, produced by an Australian manufacturer, without the patented 'kink' feature.)

Permitted 'deviation'

To describe the dimensions of Head and Handle the hockey stick is envisaged to be placed with the bottom curve of the stickhead on a level surface, the x-axis, with the stick -handle perpendicular to it (the y-axis). The y-axis runs from an intersection with the x-axis (0) vertically through the midpoint of the top of the handle. The Head is the part from the x-axis to the line C-C (diagram) a vertical distance of 100mm. This line C-C also describes the limit on any upturn to the 'toe' of the Head. By Rule there is no limit to the length of the stick-head along the x-axis, but practical considerations, as well as technicalities related to the joining of the Head and the Handle (on the line C-C), do create limitations.

The extent of the stick-head along the X+ axis, towards the 'heel' of the Head is confined by the rule requirement that the stick-head and the handle meet in a smooth continuous fashion at the line C-C and by a rule restriction on the shape of the handle, which is that the stick-handle must not project beyond the line B1-B1. It is possible to envisage a stick where the width of handle did not extend beyond the line A1-A1, thus allowing a significant extension of the stick-head along the X+ axis, but the practicalities of such a design seem to be limited and have not been explored. The length of the Head (or 'toe') along the X- axis has varied enormously, especially since the Second World War and again after the introduction of the timber lamination process in the early 1980's.

The stick handle may be bent or 'deviated', in a smooth curve only, once only to either side. That is the handle may have one outmoving curve on the 'heel' side of the head and one outmoving curve on the 'toe' side. It is therefore possible to have a hockey stick with a handle deviation to the front or 'toe' side or a handle deviation to the back or 'heel' side or a stick-handle that is bent once to both the 'toe' and 'heel' sides.

The maximum permitted width of the handle (51mm) is illustrated in the diagram by the distance between the dotted lines A-A and A1-A1. A hockey stick handle will rarely be of the maximum permitted width: most are between 46mm and 48mm at the widest point.

The maximum permitted 'deviation' is shown by the lines B-B and B1-B1 respectively. The line B-B is 20mm further along the X- axis than the line A-A and the line B1-B1 is 20mm further along the X+ axis than the line A1-A1. There is no limit along the y-axis specified, so the deviation curve or curves may be of any length along the length of the stick-handle and some goalkeeping sticks have an outward curve on the 'toe' side that extends for almost half the total length of the stick.

Permitted bow

Increasing the degree of bow to the 'face' side (flat side) makes it easier to get high speeds from the drag-flick (a 'sling-shot' style stroke started from behind the body of the flicker) and allows easier execution of the stroke. At first, after extreme bows where introduced (2005), the Hockey Rules Board (HRB) placed a limit of 50mm on the maximum depth of such a bow over the length of the stick, but experience quickly demonstrated this degree of bend to be excessive.

The Rules of Hockey 2006 limited this particular curve of the stick to 25mm so as to limit the power with which the ball can be flicked and to try to ensure that hitting control was maintained (the curvature to the face of the stick considerably influences the angle at which the stick-head strikes through the ball). The placement of the maximum bow along the length of the handle has not, however been specified, so the angle at which the stickhead is presented to the ball (and hence the facility to lift the ball easily) will vary (as will the propensity to lift the ball accidentally when hitting it).

It is now illegal for any hockey stick to have a bow that exceeds 25 mm. The bow height is measured by placing the stick face-side to a flat surface and presenting the official measuring device, a 25mm high metal triangular or cylindrical measure, to the gap between the surface and the under-flat of the stick. In some countries a coin of the correct diameter may be availbale for this purpose: the Austrialian dollar for example is suitable or the British pound coin (which is 26mm in diameter) can be used (unofficially) because very small distances can be very accurately estimated by eye and a difference of more than 1mm. would be easy to spot.

Forehand Striking Position

For the purposes of this article the ball will be assumed to be 73mm in diameter. Ball size does play a significant part in stickwork and ball control (as does the hardness of the ball) but an investigation of that is outside the scope of this article. The width of stick handles does vary (as does the horizontal length of stickheads) but for clarity and convenience the shaft of the handle just above the head has been taken as 46mm and the sticks scaled from that measurement.

The position of the ball when it is played, particularly hit with the stickhead, does, however have a bearing on stickhead design. Using just one of the whole range of angles the ball may be struck at from the forehand (right-hand) side (45°), the position of the ball will be looked at in relation to both the centre of the head of the stick and a line projected to run through the centre of the handle. An examination on the position of wear on the base of stickheads that have been used over a period on an abrasive playing surface lead to the conclusion that the ball is positioned close to the center of the head length of the modern stick. This is also the more usual position for receiving or stopping the ball in play while in the 'dribbling crouch'. Obviously when the handle is vertical or horizontal there is considerable variation but in most common hitting and dribbling positions the line of the uppermost edge of the handle projects close to the centre of the ball.

One of the problems with a striking head that is significantly narrower than the diameter of the ball is that the ball is easily lifted unintentionally if struck with the face of the stickhead inclined backward, 'open', rather than vertical or nearly so. Striking the ball with a 'closed' face is not always a solution, because it is then possible to 'squeeze' or 'clip' it, again causing the ball to rise, possibly even more steeply than with the so called 'undercut' hit.

Another difficulty is striking the ball accurately at the point on the stickhead that is intended (the usual range of error can be seen, in the diagram, in the difference of the lengths of the red lines that run from the centre of the two differently positioned stickheads).

It is also necessary to avoid unintentionally turning the handle during a hit at the ball so that the ball is 'sliced' (to the right) or hooked (to the left), this is achieved by gripping the stick firmly, generally with one hand locked against the other at the top of the handle, at the moment of impact with the ball.

Ensuring vertical and flat (perpendicular to intended direction of ball travell) contact with the ball is in the hands of the player and the coach, but achieving a correct contact position between the stickhead and the ball can be, to a limited extent, helped by the design of the stick.

At a common playing angle three different styles of hook stickhead present identical ball/handle relationships because the bend of the 'heel' is the same in each stick. An increase in the height of the 'toe' over the ball is very noticeable and is most pronounced in the more 'open' shape. The moderen hook does not suffer from the effects of a rotational imbalance in the head as much as the original did because stickheads are now generally tapered towards the 'toe', rather than of uniform thickness so 'toe' height is not, from a weight and rotational balance point of view, as much of an issue as it once might have been. The stickhead is also generally tapered from the mid-point of the striking area towards the bottom curve, so when the stick is in the reversed position the maximum thickness of the head is not at the highest point. This gives a more balanced rotation of the weight of the stickhead over the ball.

Some of the early hooks were actually thinner in the centre and became thicker in the 'toe'; it is likely that this was done to facilitate more powerful reversed-stick hitting of the ball but it gave the stick unusual handling chacteristics when turning it over the ball and back in 'stickwork': an 'overturing' or 'throw' of the stickhead had to be taken into account. The 'composite' stick is generally lighter than the previous wood versions and it is unusual these days to find a young player using the 25oz—26oz sticks that were quite commonly used on grass in the 1970's, especially by those likely to be regularly taking hits at a stationary ball.

Hockey Ball

The ball is hard and of plastic (sometimes over a cork core) and is often covered with indentations to reduce hydroplaning that can cause an inconsistent ball speed on wet surfaces.

General Player Equipment

Many players wear mouth guards to protect teeth and gums from impacts from the ball or stick. Some local rules require their use such as US high school competition. In these competitions, from the 2006 season, no clear or white mouth guards will be allowed; they have to be coloured, making it easier for umpires to confirm that the guards are being worn. Many players also wear shin guards, and again these may be required equipment in some areas. A few competitions, such as American high school competitions, require goggles (field hockey or lacrosse) to protect the eyes.

Goalkeeping Equipment

The 2007 rulebook has seen major changes regarding goalkeepers. A "fully-equipped goalkeeper" must wear a helmet, leg guards and kickers. Usually they wear extensive additional protective equipment including chest guards, padded shorts, heavily padded hand protectors, groin protectors, neck guards, arm guards, and like all players, must carry a stick. However, such a player may not cross the 23m line. However, if the goalkeeper elects to wear only a helmet (and a different coloured shirt), they may cross the 23m line if they have removed their helmet. If play returns to the circle without them having opportunity to replace the helmet, this player still has "goalkeeping privileges", that is, they are not limited to using their stick to play the ball whilst it is in the circle. The helmet must be worn whilst defending penalty corners and penalty strokes.

It is now also possible for teams to have a full eleven outfield players—and no goalkeeper at all. No player may wear a helmet or other goalkeeping equipment, nor will any player be able to play the ball other than with their stick. This may be used to offer a tactical advantage, or to allow for play to commence if no goalkeeper or kit is available.

Tactics

The main methods by which the ball is moved around the field by players are: the "dribble", where the player controls the ball with the stick and runs with the ball, pushing the ball along as they run; The "push", where the player uses their wrists to push at the ball; the "flick" or "scoop", similar to the push but with an additional wrist action to force the stick through at an angle and lift the ball off the ground; and the "hit", where a backlift is taken and contact with the ball is made quite forcefully.

In order to produce a much stronger hit, usually for travel over long distances, the stick is raised higher and swung at the ball, sometimes known as a "drive". Tackles are made by placing the stick into the path of the ball. To increase the effectiveness of the tackle, players will often place the entire stick close to the ground horizontally, thus representing a wider barrier. To avoid the tackle, the ball carrier will either pass the ball to a teammate using any of the push, flick, or hit, or attempt to maneuver or "pull" the ball around the tackle, trying to deceive the tackler.

When passing and maneuvering between players, certain commands are used to ensure understanding of movements and plays among teammates. Although these vary depending on which country the game is in, there are a few standard calls. By calling "through" or "straight" the ball is passed straight ahead to another player. "Flat" or "square" signifies a pass made to the right or left of the player with the ball at a 90 degree angle. Passes made backward are occasionally signified by a call of "drop". A hit made forward at an angle is recognised as "up" or "through".

In recent years, the penalty corner has gained importance as a vital part of the game as a goal scoring opportunity. Particularly with the advent and popularisation of the drag flick, penalty corners are highly sought after. Some tactics or set plays used involve the aforementioned drag flick, the straight hit, deflections towards goal, and various, more complex plays, using passes before shots at goal.

At the highest level, hockey is a fast-moving, highly skilled sport, with players using fast moves with the stick, quick accurate passing, and hard hits, in attempts to keep possession and move the ball towards the goal. While physically tackling and otherwise obstructing players is not permitted, collisions are common, and the speed at which the ball travels along the ground (and sometimes through the air, which is legal if it is not judged dangerous by the umpire) requires the use of padded shin guards to prevent injury. Some of the tactics used resemble football (soccer), but with greater speed—the best players maneuver and score almost quicker than the eye can see.

Formations

Formations provide structure to a hockey team on the pitch. They help players understand and share the defensive and attacking responsibilities. Although higher level teams may select from a wide range of formations, teams containing inexperienced players or teams which see frequent changes to their players are likely to select from a more limited range of formations such as 4-3-3, 5-3-2 and 4-4-2. The 2-3-5 formation, used predominantly in Australia from relatively lowly interschool to professional interstate competitions, provides common language for many players and helps explain why "centre half" is often a name used for a player in the centre of a defence with 4 or 5 players.

Because hockey teams have 1 goalkeeper plus 10 outfield players as does association football (soccer), there are many common formations between the two sports.

One important difference in modern hockey is the absence of an offside rule. This allows attackers (often a lone attacker) to play well up the pitch, stretching the opponents' defence and using the large spaces to be found there. To counter this, defences usually keep a matching number of defenders near those attackers. This can frequently lead to formations such as 1-4-4-1 which is an adaptation of 5-4-1.

International Tournaments

The biggest two field hockey tournaments are

undoubtedly the Olympic Games tournament, and the Hockey World Cup, which is also held every 4 years. Apart from this, there is the Champions Trophy held each year for the six top-ranked teams. Field hockey has also played been at the Commonwealth Games since 1998. Amongst the men, India has won 8 Olympic golds and Pakistan have lifted the World Cup 4 times. Amongst the women, Australia has 3 Olympic golds while Netherlands has clinched the World Cup 6 times. Sultan Azlan Shah Hockey Tournament held annually in Malaysia is becoming a prominent Hockey Tournament where teams from around the world participate to win the cup.

3

Playing the Game

FIELD OF PLAY

The information below provides a simplified description of the field of play. Detailed specifications of the field and equipment are provided in a separate section at the end of these Rules.

1. The field of play is rectangular, 91.40 metres long and 55.00 metres wide.
2. Side-lines mark the longer perimeters of the field ; backlines mark the shorter perimeters of the field.
3. The goal-lines are the parts of the back-lines between the goal-posts.
4. A centre-line is marked across the middle of the field.
5. Lines known as 23 metres lines are marked across the field 22.90 metres from each back-line.
6. Areas referred to as the circles are marked inside the field around the goals and opposite the centres of the backlines.
7. Penalty spots 150 mm in diameter are marked in front of the centre of each goal with the centre of each spot 6.40 metres from the inner edge of the goal-line.

8. All lines are 75 mm wide and are part of the field of play.
9. Flag-posts between 1.20 and 1.50 metres in height are placed at each corner of the field.
10. Goals are positioned outside the field of play at the centre of and touching each back-line.

COMPOSITION OF TEAMS

1. A maximum of eleven players from each team take part in play at any particular time during the match.
2. Each team has a goalkeeper on the field or plays only with field players.

   Each team may play with :

   — a goalkeeper with goalkeeping privileges wearing full protective equipment comprised of at least headgear, leg uards and kickers and a different colour shirt ; or

   — a goalkeeper with goalkeeping privileges wearing only protective headgear and a different colour shirt ; or

   — only field players and no player with goalkeeping privileges and therefore no player wearing protective headgear or different colour shirt.

A team may change between these options by making a substitution.

3. Each team is permitted to substitute from its players not on the field of play :

   a) substitution is permitted at any time except within the period from the award of a penalty corner until after it has been completed ; during this period substitution is only permitted for injury to or suspension of the defending goalkeeper

b) there is no limit to the number of players who are permitted to be substituted at the same time or to the number of times any player is permitted to substitute or be substituted

c) substitution of a player is permitted only after that player has left the field

d) substitutions are not permitted for suspended players during their suspension

e) after completing a suspension, a player is permitted to be substituted without first returning to the field

f) field players must leave or enter the field for substitution purposes within 3 metres of the centre-line on a side of the field agreed with the umpires

g) goalkeepers are permitted to leave or enter the field for substitution near the goal they are defending

h) time is stopped for substitution of goalkeepers wearing full protective equipment but not for other substitutions.

4. For substitution purposes, a penalty corner is completed when :

a) a goal is scored

b) an attacker commits an offence

c) the ball travels more than 5 metres outside the circle

d) the ball travels outside the circle for the second time

e) the ball is played over the back-line and another penalty corner is not awarded

f) a defender commits an offence and another penalty corner is not awarded

g) a penalty stroke is awarded

h) a bully is awarded.

If another penalty corner is awarded, substitution must not take place until that penalty corner has been completed.

5. Field players who leave the field for injury treatment, refreshment, to change equipment or for some reason other than substitution are only permitted to re-enter between the 23 metres areas.

6. No persons other than field players, goalkeepers and umpires are permitted on the field during the match without the permission of an umpire.

7. Players on or off the field are under the jurisdiction of the umpires throughout the match including the half-time interval.

8. A player who is injured or bleeding must leave the field unless medical reasons prevent this and must not return until wounds have been covered ; players must not wear blood stained clothing.

Captains

1. One player of each team must be appointed as captain.

2. A replacement captain must be appointed when a captain is suspended.

3. Captains must wear a distinctive arm-band or similar distinguishing article on an upper arm or shoulder.

4. Captains are responsible for the behaviour of all players on their team and for ensuring that

substitutions of players on their team are carried out correctly.

A personal penalty is awarded if a captain does not exercise these responsibilities.

Players' Clothing and Equipment

Tournament Regulations available from the FIH provide additional information and requirements about players' clothing, personal equipment and advertising. Refer also to regulations established by Continental Federations and National Associations.

1. Field players of the same team must wear uniform clothing.
2. Players must not wear anything which is dangerous to other players.

   Field players :

   — are permitted to wear gloves for protection which do not increase the natural size of the hands significantly ;

   — are recommended to wear shin, ankle and mouth protection ;

   — are permitted to wear throughout a match for medical reasons only a smooth preferably transparent or white but otherwise dark plain coloured face mask which fits.ush with the face, soft protective head-covering or eye protection in the form of plastic goggles (ie goggles with a soft-covered frame and plastic lenses) ; the medical reasons must be assessed by an appropriate authority and the player concerned must understand the possible implications of playing with the medical condition ;

   — are permitted to wear a smooth preferably transparent or white but otherwise dark plain coloured face mask which.ts.ush with the face when defending a penalty corner or penalty stroke for the duration of that penalty corner or penalty stroke ;

— are not be permitted to wear protective headgear (face mask or other protective head covering) in any other circumstances.

3. Goalkeepers must wear over any upper body protection a shirt or garment which is different in colour from that of both teams.

4. Goalkeepers must wear :

   a protective equipment comprised of at least headgear, leg guards and kickers except that the headgear and any hand protectors may be removed when taking a penalty stroke or, if the team has chosen this option

   b only protective headgear.

   Protective headgear incorporating a helmet with fixed full-face protection and cover for the entire head and throat is recommended for goalkeepers.

   The following are permitted for use only by fully equipped goalkeepers : body, upper arm, elbow, forearm, hand and thigh protectors, leg guards and kickers.

5. Clothing or protective equipment which significantly increases the natural size of a goalkeeper's body or area of protection is not permitted.

6. The stick has a traditional shape with a handle and a curved head which is flat on its left side :

   a) the stick must be smooth and must not have any rough or sharp parts

   b) inclusive of any additional coverings used, the

stick must be able to pass through a ring with an interior diameter of 51 mm

c) any curvature along the length of the stick (the rake or bow) must have a continuous smooth profile along the whole length, must occur along the face side or the back of the stick but not both and is limited to a depth of 25 mm

d) the stick must conform with the specification agreed by the Hockey Rules Board.

7. The ball is spherical, hard and white (or an agreed colour which contrasts with the playing surface).

Detailed specifications of the stick, ball and goalkeeper's equipment are provided in a separate section at the end of these Rules.

Match and Result

1. A match consists of two periods of 35 minutes and a halftime interval of 5 minutes.

   Other periods and interval may be agreed by both teams except as specified in regulations for particular competitions.

2. The team scoring the most goals is the winner ; if no goals are scored, or if the teams score an equal number of goals, the match is drawn.

   Information about extra time and a penalty stroke competition as ways of reaching a result in a drawn match is included in Tournament Regulations available from the FIH Office.

Start and Re-start the Match

1. A coin is tossed :

   a) the team which wins the toss has the choice of which goal to attack in the first half of the match or to start the match with a centre pass

b) if the team winning the toss chooses which goal to attack in the first half of the match, the opposing team starts the match

c) if the team winning the toss chooses to start the match, the opposing team has the choice of which goal to attack in the first half of the match.

2. Direction of play is reversed in the second half of the match.

3. A centre pass is taken :

a) to start the match by a player from the team winning the toss if they chose this option ; otherwise by a player from the opposing team

b) to re-start the match after half-time by a player of the team which did not take the centre pass to start the match

c) after a goal by a player of the team against which the goal was scored or awarded.

4. Taking a centre pass :

a) taken at the centre of the field

b) it is permitted to play the ball in any direction

c) all players other than the player taking the centre pass must be in the half of the field which includes the goal they are defending

d) the procedures for taking a free hit apply.

5. A bully takes place to re-start a match when time or play has been stopped for an injury or for any other reason and no penalty has been awarded :

a) a bully is taken close to the location of the ball when play was stopped but not within 15 metres of the backline

b) the ball is placed between one player from each team who face each other with the goal they are defending to their right

c) the two players start with their sticks on the ground to the right of the ball and then tap the fiat faces of their sticks together once just over the ball after which either player is permitted to play the ball

d) all other players must be at least 5 metres from the ball.

6. A free hit is taken by a defender 15 metres in front of the centre of the goal-line to re-start a match when a penalty stroke has been completed and no goal has been scored or awarded.

BALL OUTSIDE THE FIELD

1. The ball is out of play when it passes completely over the side-line or back-line.
2. Play is restarted by a player of the team which did not touch or play the ball immediately before it went out of play.
3. When the ball travels over the side-line, play is re-started where the ball crossed the line and the procedures for taking a free hit apply.
4. When the ball is played over the back-line and no goal is scored :

a) if played by an attacker, play is re-started with the ball up to 15 metres from and in line with where it crossed the back-line and the procedures for taking a free hit apply

b) if played unintentionally by a defender or deflected by a goalkeeper, play is re-started with the ball on the mark 5 metres from the corner of the field on the side-line nearest to where the ball crossed the back-line and the procedures for taking a free hit apply

c) if played intentionally by a defender, unless deflected by a goalkeeper, play is re-started with a penalty corner.

Method of scoring

1. A goal is scored when the ball is played within the circle by an attacker and does not travel outside the circle before passing completely over the goal-line and under the cross-bar.

   The ball may be played by a defender or touch their body before or after being played in the circle by an attacker.

2. A goal is scored if awarded as a result of a penalty stroke.

Conduct of play : players

Players are expected to act responsibly at all times.

1. A match is played between two teams with not more than eleven players of each team on the field at the same time.
2. Players on the field must hold their stick and not use it in a dangerous way.

   Players must not lift their stick over the heads of other players.

3. Players must not touch, handle or interfere with other players or their sticks or clothing.
4. Players must not intimidate or impede another player.
5. Players must not play the ball with the back of the stick.

6. Players must not hit the ball hard on the forehand with the edge of the stick.

   This does not prohibit use of the edge of the stick on the forehand in a controlled action in a tackle, when raising the ball in a controlled way over an opponent's stick or over a goalkeeper who is lying on the ground or when using a long pushing motion along the ground.

   The use of the edge of the stick on the backhand has developed as a technical skill and is permitted subject to danger.

7. Players must not play the ball with any part of the stick when the ball is above shoulder height except that defenders are permitted to use the stick to stop or deflect a shot at goal at any height.

   When saving a shot at goal, a defender must not be penalised if their stick is not motionless or is travelling towards the ball while attempting to stop or deflect the shot. Only if the ball is genuinely hit while above shoulder height and a goal is prevented should a penalty stroke be awarded. If a defender attempts to stop or deflect a ball travelling towards the goal which will actually miss the goal, any use of the stick above the shoulder must be penalised by a penalty corner and not a penalty stroke.

   If dangerous play results after a legitimate stop or deflection, a penalty corner must be awarded.

8. Players must not play the ball dangerously or in a way which leads to dangerous play.

   A ball is considered dangerous when it causes legitimate evasive action by players.

   The penalty is awarded where the action causing the danger took place.

9. Players must not intentionally raise the ball from a hit except for a shot at goal.

   A raised hit must be judged explicitly on whether or not it is raised intentionally. It is not an offence to raise the ball unintentionally from a hit, including a free hit, anywhere on the field unless it is dangerous.

   If the ball is raised over an opponent's stick or body on the ground, even within the circle, it is permitted unless judged to be dangerous.

   Players are permitted to raise the ball with a.ick or scoop provided it is not dangerous. A.ick or scoop towards an opponent within 5 metres is considered dangerous. If an opponent is clearly running into the shot or into the attacker without attempting to play the ball with their stick, they should be penalised for dangerous play.

10. Players must not approach within 5 metres of an opponent receiving a falling raised ball until it has been received, controlled and is on the ground.

    The initial receiver has a right to the ball. If it is not clear which player is the initial receiver, the player of the team which raised the ball must allow the opponent to receive it.

11. Field players must not stop, kick, propel, pick up, throw or carry the ball with any part of their body.

    It is not always an offence if the ball hits the foot, hand or body of a field player. The player only commits an offence if they voluntarily use their hand, foot or body to play the ball or if they position themselves with the intention of stopping the ball in this way.

It is not an offence if the ball hits the hand holding the stick but would otherwise have hit the stick.

12. Players must not obstruct an opponent who is attempting to play the ball.

Players obstruct if they :

— back into an opponent
— physically interfere with the stick or body of an opponent
— shield the ball from a legitimate tackle with their stick or any part of their body.

A stationary player receiving the ball is permitted to face in any direction.

A player with the ball is permitted to move off with it in any direction except bodily into an opponent.

A player who runs in front of or blocks an opponent to stop them legitimately playing or attempting to play the ball is obstructing (this is third party or shadow obstruction). This also applies if an attacker runs across or blocks defenders (including the goalkeeper) when a penalty corner is being taken.

13. Players must not tackle unless in a position to play the ball without body contact.

14. Players must not intentionally enter the goal their opponents are defending or run behind either goal.

15. Players must not force an opponent into offending unintentionally.

Playing the ball clearly and intentionally into any part of an opponent's body may be penalised as an attempt to manufacture an offence. Forcing an opponent to obstruct (often emphasised by running into an opponent or by waving the stick) must also be penalised.

16. Players must not change their stick between the award and completion of a penalty corner or penalty stroke unless it no longer meets the stick specification.
17. Players must not throw any object or piece of equipment onto the field, at the ball, or at another player, umpire or person.
18. Players must not delay play to gain benefit by timewasting.

Conduct of play : goalkeepers

1. A goalkeeper who :
   a) wears protective equipment comprised of at least headgear, leg guards and kickers must not take part in the match outside the 23 metres area they are defending, except when taking a penalty stroke
   b) wears only protective headgear must not take part in the match outside the 23 metres area they are defending when wearing the headgear but may remove the headgear and take part in the match anywhere on the field.

   The protective headgear must be worn when defending a penalty corner or penalty stroke.
2. When the ball is inside the circle they are defending and they have their stick in their hand, goalkeepers are permitted to :
   a) use their stick, protective equipment or any part of their body to push the ball away, deflect the ball (in any direction including over the back-line) or stop the ball

This permits a goalkeeper to use their hands, arms or any other part of their body to move the ball away but only as part of a goal saving action and not to propel the ball forcefully so that it travels a long distance.

b) use their stick, feet, kickers, legs or leg guards to propel the ball forcefully.

3. Goalkeepers must not lie on the ball.
4. When the ball is outside the circle they are defending, goalkeepers are only permitted to play the ball with their stick.

Conduct of Play : Umpires

1. Two umpires control the match, apply the Rules and are the judges of fair play.
2. Each umpire has primary responsibility for decisions in one half of the field for the duration of the match.
3. Each umpire is responsible for decisions on free hits in the circle, penalty corners, penalty strokes and goals in one half of the field.
4. Umpires are responsible for keeping a written record of goals scored or awarded and of warning or suspension cards used.
5. Umpires are responsible for ensuring that the full time is played and for indicating the end of time for each half and for the completion of a penalty corner if a half is prolonged.
6. Umpires blow the whistle to :

   a) start and end each half of the match

   b) start a bully

   c) enforce a penalty

   d) start and end a penalty stroke

e) indicate a goal

f) re-start the match after a goal has been scored or awarded

g) re-start the match after a penalty stroke when a goal was not scored or awarded

h) stop the match for the substitution of a goalkeeper and to restart the match on completion of the substitution

i) stop the match for any other reason and to re-start it j indicate, when necessary, that the ball has passed wholly outside the field.

7. Umpires must not coach during a match.

8. If the ball strikes an umpire, unauthorised person or any loose object on the field, play continues.

Penalties

1. Advantage : a penalty is awarded only when a player or team has been disadvantaged by an opponent breaking the Rules.

   If awarding a penalty is not an advantage to the team which did not break the Rules, play must continue.

2. A free hit is awarded to the opposing team :

   a) for an offence by any player between the 23 metres areas

   b) for an offence by an attacker within the 23 metres area their opponents are defending

   c) for an unintentional offence by a defender outside the circle but within the 23 metres area they are defending.

3. A penalty corner is awarded :

a) for an offence by a defender in the circle which does not prevent the probable scoring of a goal

b) for an intentional offence in the circle by a defender against an opponent who does not have possession of the ball or an opportunity to play the ball

c) for an intentional offence by a defender outside the circle but within the 23 metres area they are defending

d) for intentionally playing the ball over the back-line by a defender

Goalkeepers are permitted to deflect the ball with their stick, protective equipment or any part of their body in any direction including over the back-line.

e) when the ball becomes lodged in a player's clothing or equipment while in the circle they are defending.

4. A penalty stroke is awarded :

a) for an offence by a defender in the circle which prevents the probable scoring of a goal

b) for an intentional offence in the circle by a defender against an opponent who has possession of the ball or an opportunity to play the ball

c) for defenders persistently crossing over the back-line before permitted during the taking of penalty corners.

5. If there is another offence or misconduct before the awarded penalty has been taken :

a) a free hit may be progressed up to 10 metres

A free hit to the attack cannot be progressed to inside the circle.

b) a more severe penalty may be awarded

c) a personal penalty may be awarded

d) the penalty may be reversed if the subsequent offence was committed by the team first awarded the penalty.

PROCEDURES FOR TAKING PENALTIES

1. Location of a free hit :

a) a free hit is taken close to where the offence occurred

'Close to' means within playing distance of where the offence occurred and with no significant advantage gained.

The location from which a free hit is taken must be more precise inside the 23 metres area especially when the offence occurs close to the circle.

A free hit to the attacking team a small distance outside the circle must not be dragged inside the circle ; the ball must leave the stick before entering the circle.

b) a free hit awarded outside the circle to the defence within 15 metres of the back-line is taken up to 15 metres from the back-line in line with the location of the offence, parallel to the side-line

c) a free hit awarded inside the circle to the defence is taken anywhere inside the circle or up to 15 metres from the back-line in line with the location of the offence, parallel to the side-line.

2. Procedures for taking a free hit, centre pass and putting the ball back into play after it has been outside the field :

a) the ball must be stationary

b) the ball is pushed or hit and must move at least one metre before another player of the team which took the free hit is allowed to play it

A 'dragging' action used to play the ball at a free hit must not result in playing the ball twice.

c) the ball must not be raised intentionally

d) after playing the ball, the player taking the free hit must not play the ball again or approach within playing distance of it until it has been played by another player

e) opponents must be at least 5 metres from the ball.

If a player is standing within 5 metres of the ball but not influencing play, the free hit need not be delayed.

f) when a free hit is awarded to the attack within 5 metres of the circle, all players other than the player taking the free hit must be at least 5 metres from the ball.

3. Taking a penalty corner :

a) the ball is placed on the back-line inside the circle at least 10 metres from the goal-post on whichever side of the goal the attacking team prefers

b) an attacker pushes or hits the ball without intentionally raising it

c) the attacker taking the push or hit from the back-line must have at least one foot outside the field

d) the other attackers must be on the field, outside the circle with sticks, hands and feet not touching the ground inside the circle

e) no defender or attacker other than the attacker taking the push or hit from the back-line is permitted to be within 5 metres of the ball when the push or hit is taken

f) not more than five defenders, including the goalkeeper if there is one, must be positioned behind the backline with their sticks, hands and feet not touching the ground inside the field

If the team defending a penalty corner has chosen to play only with field players, none of the defenders referred to above has goalkeeping privileges.

g) the other defenders must be beyond the centre-line

h) until the ball has been played, no attacker other than the one taking the push or hit from the back-line is permitted to enter the circle and no defender is permitted to cross the centre-line or back-line

i) after playing the ball, the attacker taking the push or hit from the back-line must not play the ball again or approach within playing distance of it until it has been played by another player

j) a goal cannot be scored until the ball has travelled outside the circle

k) if the first shot at goal is a hit (as opposed to a push, fiick or scoop), the ball must cross the goal-line, or be on a path which would have resulted in it crossing the goal-line, at a height of not more than 460 mm (the height of the backboard) before any deflection, for a goal to be scored

The requirements of this Rule apply even if the ball touches the stick or body of a defender before the first shot at goal.

If the first shot at goal is a hit and the ball is, or will be, too high crossing the goal-line it must be penalised even if the ball is subsequently deflected off the stick or body of another player.

The ball may be higher than 460 mm during its.ight before it crosses the goal-line provided there is no danger and provided it would drop of its own accord below 460 mm before crossing the line.

'Slap' hitting the ball, which involves a long pushing or sweeping movement with the stick before making contact with the ball, is regarded as a hit.

l) for second and subsequent hits at the goal and for.icks, deflections and scoops, it is permitted to raise the ball to any height but this must not be dangerous

A defender who is clearly running into the shot or into the taker without attempting to play the ball with their stick must be penalised for dangerous play.

Otherwise, if a defender is within five metres of the first shot at goal during the taking of a penalty corner and is struck by the ball below the knee, another penalty corner must be awarded or is struck above the knee in a normal stance, the shot is judged to be dangerous and a free hit must be awarded to the defending team.

m) the penalty corner Rules no longer apply if the ball travels more than 5 metres from the circle.

4. The match is prolonged at half-time and full-time to

allow completion of a penalty corner or any subsequent penalty corner or penalty stroke ; for this purpose, the penalty corner is completed when :

a) a goal is scored

b) an attacker commits an offence

c) the ball travels more than 5 metres outside the circle

d) the ball travels outside the circle for the second time

e) the ball is played over the back-line and a penalty corner is not awarded

f) a defender commits an offence which does not result in another penalty corner

g) a penalty stroke is awarded.

If play is stopped during the taking of a penalty corner because of an injury or for any other reason and a bully would otherwise be awarded, the penalty corner must be taken again.

5. Taking a penalty stroke :

a) time and play is stopped when a penalty stroke is awarded

b) all players on the field other than the player taking the stroke and the player defending it must stand outside the 23 metres area and must not infiuence the taking of the stroke

c) the ball is placed on the penalty spot

d) the player taking the stroke must stand behind and within playing distance of the ball before beginning thestroke

e) the player defending the stroke must stand with both feet on the goal-line and must not leave the goal-line or move either foot until the ball has been played

f) if the player defending the stroke is a goalkeeper, they must wear protective headgear ; if the player defending the stroke is otherwise taking part in the game as a field player, they may wear only a face mask as protective equipment

If the team defending a penalty stroke has chosen to play only with field players and not to use a substitute goalkeeper to defend the penalty stroke, the defender may only use their stick to make a save.

g) the whistle is blown when the player taking the stroke and the player defending it are in position

h) the player taking the stroke must not take it until the whistle has been blown

The player taking the stroke or the player defending it must not delay the taking of the stroke.

i) the player taking the stroke must not feint at playing the ball

j) the player taking the stroke must push, fiick or scoop the ball and is permitted to raise it to any height

Using a 'dragging' action to play the ball at a penalty stroke is not permitted.

k) the player taking the stroke must play the ball only once and must not subsequently approach either the ball or the player defending the stroke.

6. The penalty stroke is completed when :

a) a goal is scored or awarded

b) the ball comes to rest inside the circle, lodges in

the goalkeeper's equipment, is caught by the goalkeeper, or goes outside the circle.

7 For an offence during the taking of a penalty stroke:

a) by the player taking the stroke : a free hit is awarded to the defence

b) when the player defending the stroke prevents a goal being scored but leaves the goal-line or moves either foot before the ball has been played : the penalty stroke is taken again

For the first offence of this type, the player must be warned (green card) and for any subsequent offence must be suspended (yellow card).

c) for any other offence by the player defending the stroke which prevents a goal being scored : a goal is awarded

d) for an offence by the player defending the stroke which does not prevent a goal being scored : the penalty stroke is taken again

e) for an offence by a player of the defending team and a goal is not scored : the penalty stroke is taken again

f) for an offence by a player of the attacking team and a goal is scored : the penalty stroke is taken again.

Personal Penalties

1. For any offence, the offending player may be :

a) cautioned (indicated by spoken words)

b) warned (indicated by a green card)

c) temporarily suspended for a minimum of 5 minutes of playing time (indicated by a yellow card)

For the duration of each temporary suspension of a player on or off the field, the offending team plays with one less player.

d) permanently suspended from the current match (indicated by a red card).

For each permanent suspension, the offending team plays for the remainder of the match with one less player.

A personal penalty may be awarded in addition to the appropriate penalty.

2. Temporarily suspended players must remain in a designated place until permitted by the umpire who suspended them to resume play.
3. Temporarily suspended players are permitted to rejoin their team at half-time after which they must return to a designated place to complete their suspension.
4. The intended duration of a temporary suspension may be extended for misconduct by a player while suspended.
5. Permanently suspended players must leave the field and its surrounding area.

4

Umpiring

Objectives

1. Umpiring hockey is a challenging but rewarding way to participate in the game.
2. Umpires contribute to the game by :
   a) helping to raise the standard of the game at all levels by ensuring that players observe the Rules
   b) ensuring that every game is played in the right spirit
   c) helping to increase the enjoyment of the game for players, spectators, and others.
3. These objectives can be achieved by umpires being :
   a) consistent : umpires maintain the respect of players by being consistent
   b) fair : decisions must be made with a sense of justice and integrity
   c) prepared : no matter how long an umpire has been officiating, it is important to prepare thoroughly for every match
   d) focused : concentration must be maintained at all times ; nothing must be allowed to distract an umpire

e) approachable : a good understanding of the Rules must be combined with a good rapport with the players

f) better : umpires must aim to become even better with each and every match

g) natural : an umpire must be themselves, and not imitate another person, at all times.

4. Umpires must :

a) have a thorough knowledge of the Rules of Hockey but remember that the spirit of the Rule and common sense must govern interpretation

b) support and encourage skilful play, deal promptly and firmly with offences and apply the appropriate penalties

c) establish control and maintain it throughout the match

d) use all the available tools for control

e) apply the advantage Rule as much as possible to assist a flowing and open match but without losing control.

Applying the Rules

1. Protecting skilful play and penalising offences :

a) the relative seriousness of an offence must be identified and serious offences such as dangerous or rough play dealt with early and firmly in a match

b) intentional offences must be penalised firmly

c) umpires must demonstrate that if players co-operate, skilful play will be protected and the match will be interrupted only when essential for its proper conduct.

2. Advantage :

   a) it is not necessary for every offence to be penalised when no benefit is gained by the offender ; unnecessary interruptions to the flow of the match cause undue delay and irritation

   b) when the Rules have been broken, an umpire must apply advantage if this is the most severe penalty

   c) possession of the ball does not automatically mean there is an advantage ; for advantage to apply, the player/team with the ball must be able to develop their play

   d) having decided to play advantage, a second opportunity must not be given by reverting to the original penalty

   e) it is important to anticipate the flow of the match, to look beyond the action of the moment and to be aware of potential developments in the match.

3. Control :

   a) decisions must be made promptly, positively, clearly and consistently

   b) strict action early in a match will usually discourage repetition of an offence

   c) it is not acceptable for players to abuse opponents, umpires or other technical officials verbally or through body language and attitude. Umpires must deal firmly with abuse of this sort and in appropriate circumstances issue a caution, warning (green card), or a temporary (yellow card) or permanent (red card) suspension. Cautions, warnings and suspensions can be given in isolation or in combination with another penalty

d) cautions can be given to players in close proximity without stopping the match

e) it is possible for a player to receive two green or two yellow cards for different offences during the same match but when an offence for which a card has been awarded is repeated, the same card must not be used again and a more severe penalty must be awarded

f) when a second yellow card is awarded, the period of suspension must be significantly longer than the first suspension

g) there must be a clear difference between the duration of a yellow card suspension for a minor offence and the duration for a more serious and/or physical offence

h) when a player intentionally misbehaves in a serious manner towards another player, umpire or other match official the red card must be shown immediately.

4. Penalties :

a) a wide range of penalties is available

b) two penalties can be used together to deal with bad or persistent offences.

Umpiring skills

1. The main umpiring skill areas are :

a) match preparation

b) co-operation

c) mobility and positioning

d) whistling

e) signalling.

2. Match preparation :

   a) umpires must prepare thoroughly for each match by arriving at the field in good time

   b) before the match commences, both umpires must check the field markings, the goals and the nets and check for any dangerous playing equipment or field equipment

   c) the two umpires must wear similar colours to one another, but different from those of both teams

   d) clothing appropriate to the conditions must be worn

   e) footwear must suit field conditions and assist mobility

   f) umpiring equipment includes a copy of the current Rules book, a loud and distinctive whistle, a stop watch, coloured cards to indicate personal penalties and materials to record match details.

3. Co-operation :

   a) good team-work and co-operation between umpires is essential

   b) prior to a match, umpires must discuss and agree how they are going to work together to assist each other. Eye contact between umpires must be practised and maintained

   c) umpires must take responsibility and be prepared to assist when their colleague is unsighted or has difficulty seeing certain parts of the field. If necessary and if mobility is good, umpires must be prepared to cross the centre-line and go as far as appropriate into a colleague's half of the field to assist. This helps to reassure players that decisions are correct

d) a written record of goals scored and cards issued must be kept by both umpires and confirmed at the end of the match.

4. Mobility and positioning :

a) umpires must be mobile so they can move to appropriate positions throughout the match.

b) static umpires cannot view play clearly enough to make correct decisions at all times

c) fit, mobile and well positioned umpires are better able to concentrate on the flow of the match and on the decisions which need to be made

d) each umpire operates mainly in half of the field with the centre line to their left

e) in general, the most suitable position for umpires is ahead of and on the right of the attacking team

f) for play between the centre-line and 23 metres area, umpires must be positioned near their side-line

g) when play is in the 23 metres area or circle, umpires must move further into the field away from the sidelines and, when necessary, into the circle itself to see important offences and to judge whether shots at goal are legitimate

h) for penalty corners and after the ball has gone outside the field, umpires must take up a position which gives a clear view of all potential action

i) for penalty strokes, umpires must take up a position behind and to the right of the player taking the stroke

j) umpires must not allow their positioning to

interfere with the flow of play k umpires must face the players all the time.

5 Whistling :

a) the whistle is the main way in which umpires communicate with players, each other and other persons involved in the match

b) the whistle must be blown decisively and loudly enough for all involved in the match to be able to hear it. This does not mean long loud whistling at all times

c) the tone and duration of the whistle must be varied to communicate the seriousness of offences to players.

6. Signalling :

a) signals must be clear and held up long enough to ensure that all players and the other umpire are aware of decisions

b) only the official signals must be used

c) it is preferable to be stationary when giving a signal

d) directional signals must not be made across the body

e) it is bad practice to look away from the players when a signal or decision is made ; further offences might be missed, concentration can be lost, or this can indicate a lack of confidence.

Umpiring signals

1. Timing :

a) start time : turn towards the other umpire with one arm straight up in the air

b) stop time : turn towards the other umpire and cross fully-extended arms at the wrists above the head

c) two minutes of play remaining : raise both hands straight up in the air with pointing index fingers

d) one minute of play remaining : raise one hand straight up in the air with pointing index finger.

Once a timing signal has been acknowledged no further time signal is needed.

2. Bully : move hands alternately up and down in front of the body with palms facing each other.

3. Ball out of play :

a) ball out of play over the side-line : indicate the direction with one arm raised horizontally

b) ball out of play over the back-line by an attacker : face the centre of the field and extend both arms horizontally sideways

c) ball out of play over the back-line unintentionally by a defender : point one arm at the corner flag nearest where the ball crossed the back-line.

4. Goal scored : point both arms horizontally towards the centre of the field.

5. Conduct of play :

Signals for conduct of play offences must be shown if there is doubt about the reason for the decision.

a) dangerous play : place one forearm diagonally across the chest

b) misconduct and/or bad temper : stop play and make a calming movement by moving both hands slowly up and down, palms downward, in front of the body

c) kick : slightly raise a leg and touch it near the foot or ankle with the hand

d) raised ball : hold palms facing each other horizontally in front of the body, with one palm approximately 150 mm above the other

e) obstruction : hold crossed forearms in front of the chest

f) third party or shadow obstruction : alternately open and close crossed forearms in front of the chest

g) stick obstruction : hold one arm out and downwards in front of the body half-way between vertical and horizontal ; touch the forearm with the other hand

h) 5 metres distance : extend one arm straight up in the air showing an open hand with all fingers extended.

6. Penalties :

a) advantage : extend one arm high from the shoulder in the direction in which the benefiting team is playing

b) free hit : indicate the direction with one arm raised horizontally

c) free hit progressed up to 10 metres : raise one arm vertically with fist clenched

d) penalty corner : point both arms horizontally towards the goal

e) penalty stroke : point one arm at the penalty stroke mark and the other straight up in the air; this signal also indicates time stopped.

5

Field and Equipment Specification

Diagrams are provided to assist interpretation of these specifications but they are not necessarily drawn to scale. The text is the definitive specification.

FIELD AND FIELD EQUIPMENT

— The field of play is rectangular, 9.40 metres long bounded by side-lines and 55 metres wide bounded by back-lines.

The playing surface must continue (to create "run-off" areas) for a minimum of 2 metres at the back-lines and 1 metre at the side-lines with an additional unobstructed 1 metre in each case (that is, a total of 3 metres at the ends and 2 metres at the sides of the field). These are minimum requirements with the respective recommended areas being 3 plus 2 metres and 3 plus 1 metres (that is, a total of 5 metres at the ends and 4 metres at the sides of the field).

2. Markings :

a) no marks other than those described in this Rule are to be made on the playing surface

b) lines are 75 mm wide and must be clearly marked along their entire length

c) the side-lines and back-lines and all markings enclosed between them are part of the field

d) all marks must be made in white.

3. Lines and other marks :

a) side-lines : 91.40 metres long perimeter lines

b) back-lines : 55.00 metres long perimeter lines

c) goal-lines : the parts of the back-lines between the goal-posts

d) centre-line : across the middle of the field

e) 22.90 metres lines across the field 22.90 metres from each back-line as measured between the furthest edges of each line

The areas enclosed by and including the 22.90 metres lines, the relevant part of the side-lines, and the back-line are known as the 23 metres areas.

f) lines 300 mm long marked outside the field on each side-line with the further edge of the lines 14.63 metres from and parallel to the outer edge of the back-lines

g) lines 300 mm long marked outside the field on each side-line with the further edge of the lines 5 metres from and parallel to the outer edge of the back-lines

h) lines 300 mm long marked outside the field on each back-line on both sides of the goal at 5 metres and 10 metres from the outer edge of the nearer goal-post, as measured between the furthest edges of each line

The markings described in Rules 1.3 f, g and h were moved from inside to outside the field with effect from 2001. The distances in Rule 1.3

h were converted to metric at the same time. These revised markings apply to all new and re-marked fields. However, existing fields with the previously specified markings may continue to be used.

i) lines 150 mm long marked outside the field on each back-line 1.83 metres from the centre of the back-line, as measured between the nearest edges of these lines

j) penalty spots 150 mm in diameter marked in front of the centre of each goal with the centre of each spot 6.40 metres from the inner edge of the goal-line.

4. Circles :

a) lines 3.66 metres long and parallel to the back-lines are marked inside the field with their centres in line with the centres of the back-lines ; the distance from the outside edges of these 3.66 metres lines to the outside edges of the back-lines is 14.63 metres

b) these lines are continued in uninterrupted arcs in both directions to meet the back-lines in the form of quartercircles with centres at the inside front corner of the nearer goal-posts

c) the 3.66 metres line and the arcs are called the circlelines ; the spaces enclosed by these lines, including the lines themselves, are called the circles

d) broken lines are marked with their outer edges 5 metres from the outer edge of each circle-line ; each broken line starts with a solid section at the top centre of the circle-line and each solid section is 300 mm long with gaps between the solid sections 3 metres long

These broken lines became mandatory for international matches with effect from 1 June 2000. Their adoption for other matches is at the discretion of National Associations.

5. Goals :

   a) two vertical goal-posts joined by a horizontal crossbar are placed at the centre of each back-line on the external marks

   b) the goal-posts and cross-bar are white, rectangular in cross section, 50 mm wide and between 50 mm and 75 mm deep

   c) the goal-posts must not extend vertically beyond the cross-bar and the cross-bar must not extend horizontally beyond the goal-posts

   d) the distance between the inner edges of the goal-posts is 3.66 metres and the distance from the lower edge of the cross-bar to the ground is 2.14 metres

   e) the space outside the field, behind the goal-posts and cross-bar and enclosed by the net, side-boards and backboard is a minimum of 0.90 metres deep at the cross-bar and a minimum of 1.20 metres deep at ground-level.

6. Side-boards and back-boards :

   a) side-boards are 460 mm high and a minimum of 1.20 metres long

   b) back-boards are 460 mm high and 3.66 metres long

   c) side-boards are positioned on the ground at right angles to the back-line and are fixed to the back of the goal-posts without increasing their width

   d) back-boards are positioned on the ground at

right angles to the side-boards and parallel to the back-line, and are fixed to the end of the side-boards

e) side-boards and back-boards are of a dark colour on the inside.

7. Nets :

a) the maximum mesh size is 45 mm

b) attachment to the back of the goal-posts and cross-bar is at intervals of not more than 150 mm

c) the nets hang outside the side-boards and back-board

d) the nets are secured so as to prevent the ball passing between the net and the goal-posts, cross-bar, sideboards and back-boards

e) the nets are fitted loosely to prevent the ball rebounding.

8. Flag-posts :

a) flag-posts are between 1.20 and 1.50 metres in height

b) flag-posts are placed at each corner of the field

c) flag-posts must not be dangerous

d) if unbreakable, flag-posts must be attached to a springn base

e) flag-posts carry flags, not exceeding 300 mm in width or length.

STICK

All measurements are made and other specifications assessed with any coverings or additional fixings attached to the stick.

1. The stick :

a) the stick has a traditional shape which will be retained

b) no particular handle or head shape or design has been approved, but the introduction of extreme shapes or designs outside the specified parameters will not be permitted.

2. Diagrams of the stick :

a) descriptions and specifications

b) the stick comprises two identifiable parts, the handle and the head

c) the handle in vertical position, in the main perpendicular to a level horizontal surface (the X-axis)

d) the curved base of the head is shown placed on the Xaxis, which is the start of its vertical length (the Y-axis)

e) the head terminates at a line C - C drawn parallel to the X-axis, 100 mm along the Y-axis, in a positive direction (towards Y+)

f) the Y-axis is perpendicular to the X-axis ; for measurement purposes the stick is aligned so that the Y-axis passes through the centre of the top of the handle

g) the handle starts at the line C - C and continues in the direction Y+.

3. Shape and dimensions of the stick :

a) the entire stick must be smooth and must not have any rough or sharp parts

b) the handle and head must be of one smooth continuous cross-section along the line C - C

c) the head must be a 'J' or 'U' shape the upturned or open end of which is limited by the line C - C

d) the head is not limited along the X-axis

e) the head must be fiat on the left hand side only (the side which is to the player's left when the stick is held with the open end of the head pointing directly away from the player's front, i.e. the side shown in the diagrams)

f) the fiat playing side of the head of the stick and any continuation of it along the handle must be smooth and in a single plane with any convex or concave deviation across that plane being no more than 4 mm in any direction

Deviation across the playing side of the head of the stick is tested by placing a straight edge across this side at any point along the head and using a standard pointed depth gauge. The depth of concave curvature below the straight edge must not exceed 4 mm ; the sum of depths below the straight edge at the edges of the stick must not exceed 8 mm.

g) inclusive of any additional coverings used, the stick must be able to pass through a ring with an interior diameter of 51 mm

h) the lines A - A and A1 - A1 in the diagrams are 51 mm apart parallel to and equidistant from the Y-axis

i) the lines B - B and B1 - B1 are 20 mm from A - A and A1 - A1 respectively

j) it is permitted for the handle to be bent or curved to protrude beyond the line A - A once only along the length of the Y-axis, to the limiting line B - B at maximum

The shape and dimensions of the stick are tested using a fiat surface marked. The stick is laid playing side downwards on the surface.

k) any curvature along the length of the stick (the rake or bow) must have a continuous smooth profile along the whole length, must occur along the face side or the back of the stick but not both and is limited to a depth of 25 mm.

The rake or bow is tested using a pointed wedge the point of which is 25 mm from the fiat base or using a round cylinder with a diameter of 25 mm. The stick is laid playing side downwards on a fiat surface in its natural resting position. The wedge is placed with its base on the surface or the cylinder is laid lengthwise on the surface. The wedge or the cylinder must not pass completely under the stick at any place along its length.

4. Playing side of the stick :

a) the playing side is the entire side

b) the edges and the non-playing side must be rounded and must have a continuous smooth profile.

Players must be aware that manufacturers may refuse to replace sticks which have been broken or damaged as a consequence of using the edge of the stick to hit the ball because many sticks have not been made for use in this way.

5. The total weight of the stick must not exceed 737 grams.

6. Ball speed must not be greater than 98 % of stick head speed under test conditions.

Ball speed is determined over a series of 5 tests at a stick speed of 80 km/hour in the simulator of an FIH approved laboratory. Ball speed is calculated from the time the ball passes two measuring points and is expressed as a ratio to the speci.ed stick speed.

FIH approved hockey balls are used.

The test is carried out at prevailing laboratory conditions with a temperature of approximately 20°C and relative humidity of approximately 50 %.

7. Materials :

a) the stick and possible additions may be made of or contain any material other than metal or metallic components, provided it is fit for the purpose of playing hockey and is not hazardous

b) the application of tapes and resins is permitted provided that the stick surface remains smooth and that it conforms to the stick specifications.

8. The FIH reserves the right to prohibit any stick which, in the opinion of the Hockey Rules Board, is unsafe or likely to have a detrimental impact on playing the game.

BALL

1. The ball :

a) is spherical

b) has a circumference of between 224 mm and 235 mm

c) weighs between 156 grams and 163 grams

d) is made of any material and coloured white (or an agreed colour which contrasts with the playing surface)

e) is hard with a smooth surface but indentations are permitted.

GOALKEEPER'S EQUIPMENT

1. Hand protectors :
   a) each have a maximum width of 228 mm and length of 355 mm when laid fiat, palm upwards
   b) must not have any additions to retain the stick when the stick is not held in the hand.
2. Leg guards : each have a maximum width of 300 mm when on the leg of the goalkeeper.

   The dimensions of goalkeeper's hand protectors and leg guards are measured using gauges with the relevant internal dimensions.

6

Ice Hockey

Ice hockey, often referred to simply as hockey in Canada and the United States, is a team sport played on ice. It is a speedy and physical sport. Ice hockey is most popular in areas that are sufficiently cold for natural, reliable seasonal ice cover, though with the advent of indoor artificial ice rinks it has become a year-round pastime at the amateur level in major metropolitan areas such as cities that host an NHL or other professional-league team. It is one of the four major North American professional sports, and is represented by the National Hockey League (NHL) at the highest level, and the National Women's Hockey League (NWHL), the highest level of women's ice hockey in the world. It is the official national winter sport of Canada, where the game enjoys immense popularity, and is also the most popular spectator sport in Finland. Only six of the thirty NHL franchises are based in Canada, but Canadian players outnumber Americans in the league by a ratio of almost four to one. About thirty percent of the league's players are non-North American.

The sport's popularity in the U.S. is concentrated in certain regions, notably the Northeast, the Midwest, and Alaska. This concentration helps to make ice hockey the least watched major sport in the United States, though it is by far the most watched sport in Canada. Nonetheless, in certain major U.S. cities (notably Buffalo, Detroit, Pittsburgh, Minneapolis, Chicago, Boston, New York City, Philadelphia, Tampa, Denver, San Jose and Columbus) it commands popularity levels similar to and occasionally exceeding basketball for winter sports fans. [citation needed]

While there are 64 total members of the International Ice Hockey Federation (IIHF), Canada, the Czech Republic, Finland, Russia, Slovakia, Sweden and the United States have finished in most of the coveted 1st, 2nd and 3rd places at IIHF World Championships. Of the 63 medals awarded in men's competition at the Olympic level from 1920 on, only six did not go to the one of those countries, or a former entity thereof, such as Czechoslovakia or the Soviet Union. Only one of those six medals was above bronze. Those seven nations have also captured 162 of 177 medals awarded at 59 non-Olympic IIHF World Championships, and all medals since 1954. Likewise, all nine Olympic and 27 IIHF World Women Championships medals have gone to one of those seven countries. Also deserving of mention is Switzerland, which has won two men's bronze medals at the Olympics and finished at least third seven times at the World Championships. Switzerland also maintains one of the oldest and top-rated ice hockey leagues (the Swiss Nationalliga) outside of the NHL.

History of Ice Hockey

Games between teams hitting an object with curved sticks have been played throughout history; 4000 year-old drawings at the Beni-Hasen tombs in Egypt depict a sport resembling field hockey. The 1527 Galway Statutes in Ireland made reference to "the horlinge of the litill balle with hockie stickes or staves." The etymology of the word hockey is uncertain. It may derive from the Old French word hoquet, shepherd's crook, or from the Middle Dutch word hokkie, meaning shack or doghouse, which in popular use meant goal. Many of these games were developed for fields, though where conditions allowed they were also played on ice. 17th-century Dutch paintings show townsfolk playing a hockey-like game on a frozen canal.

European immigrants brought various versions of hockey-like games to North America, such as the Scottish sport of shinty, the closely-related Irish sport of hurling, and versions of field hockey played in England. Where necessary these seem to have been adapted for icy conditions; for example, a colonial Williamsburg newspaper records hockey being played in a snow storm in Virginia. Both English- and French-speaking Canadians played hockey on frozen rivers, lakes, and ponds using cheese-cutter style skates strapped to their boots , and early paintings show "shinney", an early form of hockey with no standard rules, being played in Nova Scotia.

Author Thomas Chandler Haliburton wrote in a book of fiction, about boys from King's College School in Windsor, Nova Scotia, playing "hurley on the ice" when he was a student there around 1800 To this day, "Shinny" (derived from Shinty) is a popular Canadian term for an informal type of hockey, either on ice or as street hockey. These early games may have also absorbed the physically aggressive aspects of what the Mi'kmaq Aboriginal First Nation in Nova Scotia called dehuntshigwa'es (lacrosse).

In 1825 Sir John Franklin wrote that "The game of hockey played on the ice was the morning sport" while on Great Bear Lake during one of his Arctic expeditions. In 1843 a British Army officer in Kingston, Ontario, wrote "Began to skate this year, improved quickly and had great fun at hockey on the ice."A Boston Evening Gazette article from 1859 makes reference to an early game of hockey on ice occurring in Halifax in that year. The first game to use a "puck-like" object rather than a ball, took place in 1860 on Kingston Harbour, involving mostly Crimean War veterans.

Based on Haliburton's writings, there have been claims that modern ice hockey originated in Windsor, Nova Scotia, and was named after an individual, as in 'Colonel Hockey's game'. Proponents of this theory claim that the surname Hockey exists in the district surrounding Windsor. In 1943, the Canadian Amateur Hockey Association declared Kingston the birthplace of hockey, based on a recorded 1886 game played between students of Queen's University and the Royal Military College of Canada.

The Society for International Hockey Research has had an "origins of hockey" committee studying this debate since 2001 and they defined hockey as: "a game played on an ice rink in which two opposing teams of skaters, using curved sticks, try to drive a small disc, ball or block into or through the opposite goals."

The committee found evidence of stick and ball games played on ice on skates in Europe in the sixteenth through eighteenth centuries, and viewed these activities as being more indicative of a hockey-like game than Haliburton's reference.

They found no evidence in the Windsor position of a connection from whatever form of hockey might have been played at Long Pond to the game played elsewhere and to modern hockey. The committee viewed as conjecture the assertion that King's schoolboys introduced the game to Halifax. They noted that the assertion that hockey was not played outside Nova Scotia until 1865 overlooks diary evidence of shinny and hockey being played at Kingston in the 1840s.

The committee concluded that Dr. Vaughan and the Windsor Hockey Heritage Society had not offered credible evidence that Windsor, Nova Scotia, is the birthplace of hockey.

The committee offered no opinion on the birth date or birthplace of hockey, but took note of a game at Montreal's Victoria Skating Rink on March 3, 1875. This is the earliest eyewitness account known to the committee of a specific game of hockey in a specific place at a specific time, and with a recorded score, between two identified teams.

The word hockey is believed to have several derivations, the most common one being from an old French word "hoquet", which means curved stick, or more specifically "shepherd s crook". In Germanic languages, there is a very old root word "hok" or "hak". The meaning -- a bent or curved piece of wood or metal.

According to the Society for International Hockey Research, the word puck is derived from the Scottish and Gaelic word "puc" or the Irish word "poc", meaning to poke, punch or deliver a blow. This definition is explained in a book published in 1910 entitled "English as we Speak it in Ireland" by P.W. Joyce. It defines the word puck as "... The blow given by a hurler to the ball with his caman or hurley is always called a puck".

Modern Game

The foundation of the modern game centers on Montreal. On March 3, 1875 the first organized indoor game was played at Montreal's Victoria Skating Rink by James Creighton and several McGill University students. In 1877, several McGill students, including Creighton, Henry Joseph, Richard F. Smith, W.F. Robertson, and W.L. Murray codified seven ice hockey rules. The first ice hockey club, McGill University Hockey Club, was founded in 1877.

The game became so popular that the first "world championship" of ice hockey was featured in Montreal's annual Winter Carnival in 1883 and the McGill team captured the "Carnival Cup". Although undocumented, it is believed that during the same year, the Oxford University Ice Hockey Club was formed to play the first Ice Hockey Varsity Match against traditional rival Cambridge in St. Moritz, Switzerland. This match was won by the Oxford Dark Blues, 6-0.The first photographs and team lists date from 1895. This continues to be the oldest hockey rivalry in history.

In 1888, the new Governor General of Canada, Lord Stanley of Preston, whose sons and daughter became hockey enthusiasts, attended the Montreal Winter Carnival tournament and was impressed with the hockey spectacle. In 1892, recognizing that there was no recognition for the best team, he purchased a decorative bowl for use as a trophy. The Dominion Hockey Challenge Cup, which later became more famously known as the Stanley Cup, was first awarded in 1893 to the champion amateur team in Canada, Montreal HC. It continues to be awarded today to the National Hockey League's championship team.

By 1893, there were almost a hundred teams in Montreal alone, and leagues throughout Canada. Winnipeg hockey players had incorporated cricket pads to better protect the goaltender's legs. They also introduced the "scoop" shot, later known as the wrist shot.

1893 also saw the first ice hockey matches in the U.S., at Yale University and Johns Hopkins University. The U.S. Amateur Hockey League was founded in New York City in 1896, and the first professional team, the

Portage Lakers was formed in 1903 in Houghton, Michigan (although there had been individual professionals in Canada before this).

The five sons of Lord Stanley were instrumental in bringing ice hockey to Europe, beating a court team (which included both the future Edward VII and George V) at Buckingham Palace in 1895. By 1903 a five-team league had been founded. The Ligue Internationale de Hockey sur Glace was founded in 1908 to govern international competitions, and the first European championships were won by Great Britain in 1910. In the mid-20th century, the Ligue became the International Ice Hockey Federation.

Professional Era

Professional ice hockey has existed since after World War I. From the first professional ice hockey league based out of Michigan in the United States, it quickly grew into Canada and to many other countries, as diverse as Switzerland, Ukraine, Great Britain or even Austria.

Canada

In North America, two openly professional leagues emerged: the National Hockey Association in 1910 and the Pacific Coast Hockey Association in 1911. Beginning in 1915, these two leagues competed for the Stanley Cup. The National Hockey League was formed in November of 1917, following a dispute between NHA team owners. The new league began play in December of that year with four Canadian teams. The NHA disbanded in 1918, and the PCHA followed it in 1924. By 1926, the NHL, with ten teams, took control of the Stanley Cup and formed a Canadian and an American division.

With the growth of professionalism in Canada, a new challenge cup, the Allan Cup, was instituted for amateur players to replace the Stanley Cup. This led to the foundation of an amateur governing body, the Canadian Hockey Association, which entered the winning Canadian team for the first Olympic title in Antwerp in 1920.

On 16 February, 2005, the NHL became the first major professional team sport in North America to cancel an entire season because of a labor dispute. Play resumed again in the fall of 2005. During the dispute, controversy arose over the decision not to award the Stanley Cup; some considered this decision a violation of the terms of the Stanley Cup's handover to the NHL. Following a legal challenge, it was agreed that the Cup's trustees could award the Cup to a non-NHL team.

The official museum for the NHL is the Hockey Hall of Fame in Toronto, Canada. Ice Hockey is one of Canada's two official sports. It is officially the "winter" sport, whereas lacrosse is officially the "summer" sport.

United States

The first professional hockey league in the world was the International Professional Hockey League. It was founded in 1904 by a dentist in Michigan, Jack Gibson. While this league had folded by 1907, it was the starting of professional hockey. The United States would continue to see professional hockey with teams from the PCHL based in Seattle and Portland. When the Boston Bruins joined the NHL in 1924, the United States was finally represented in the league. It would continue to grow in the NHL until the present day where 24 of the 30 teams are based in the US. There are several other pro leagues in the US as well, notably the AHL, ECHL, CHL, and UHL.

Great Britain

Between the wars, British ice hockey grew rapidly with

new ice rinks and an influx of Canadian players. A European competition was instituted, and in the 1936 Winter Olympics at Garmisch, Germany, Great Britain won the gold medal, imposing the first ever Olympic defeat on the Canadians. However, because of the disruption of World War II and a lack of suitable venues afterwards the sport faded rapidly.

Russia

In Russia, the Russian Super League was founded in 1996, a descendant of the old Soviet League (founded in 1946). In the Soviet league, Red Army affiliated CSKA Moscow won 32 out of 46 championships. Their games are played in accordance with IIHF rules.

Czechoslovakia

In Czechoslovakia, the Czechoslovak Extraliga was the elite ice hockey league in Czechoslovakia from 1930 until 1993, when the country split into the Czech Republic and Slovakia.

In the Czech Republic, the Czech Extraliga is rooted in the Czechoslovak Extraliga. The Czech Extraliga was spun off in 1993 following the administrative break-up of Czechoslovakia. The Czech Extraliga is the highest-level ice hockey league in the Czech Republic. The name of the league is leased a general sponsor and changes frequently. In the 2003-04, 2004-05 and 2005-06 seasons it was known as the Tipsport Extraliga; for 2001-01 and 2001-02 it was called the Ceský Telecom Extraliga, and in 1999-00 the Staropramen Extraliga. During the 2006-07 season it was known as the O2 Extraliga.

In Slovakia, the Slovak Extraliga is the highest-level ice hockey league in Slovakia. The name of the league is leased to sponsor and changes frequently. From 1993/94 to 1997/98 season it was called Extraliga, then the name changed to West Extraliga until the end of 2000/01 season. In 2001/02 its name was Boss Extraliga. Since 2002/03 season to 2004/05 the name changed to ST Extraliga and in 2005/06 to T-Com Extraliga. From January 16th, 2007 the name changed to Slovnaft Extraliga when a general sponsor agreement with Slovnaft was signed. The agreement is valid until the end of 2007/08 season. The Slovak Extraliga is also rooted in the Czechoslovak Extraliga. The 1993/94 was the first season of Slovak Extraliga as Czechoslovakia split into the Czech Republic and Slovakia on January 1st, 1993.

Sweden

In Sweden, Elitserien is the highest-level professional ice hockey league. It is generally regarded as one of the top leagues of Europe, and one of the Swedish major professional sports league. Elitserien, or the Swedish Elite League, which it is often unofficially called in English,is composed of 12 teams. The first season under the name Elitserien was played in 1975-76. The Swedish ice hockey championships has been played in various forms since 1922.

Finland

In Finland, SM-liiga is the top professional ice hockey league in Finland. It was constituted in 1975 to replace SM-sarja, which was fundamentally an amateur league. SM-liiga has an agreement of cooperation with Finnish ice hockey federation Suomen Jääkiekkoliitto. SM is a common abbreviation for Suomen mestaruus, "Finnish championship". At the moment, there are 14 teams. SM-liiga was closed in 2000 so that no team can be relegated to or promoted from the lower leagues without approval of the board of SM-liiga. The board have committed themselves to promote the first winner of Mestis (the second highest competition) that meets certain standards.

Switzerland

In Switzerland, the Nationalliga A (German), or Ligue Nationale A (French) is the top tier of the Nationalliga or Ligue Nationale, the main professional ice hockey league in Switzerland. It is the oldest league remaining today, dating to 1916.

Germany

In Germany, the Deutsche Eishockey-Liga (German Hockey League, shortname DEL) is a German high-calibre ice hockey league, and has the highest number of American and Canadian players overseas. It was formed as a replacement for the Bundesliga. It dates back to 1958.

Ice hockey equipment

The hard surfaces of the ice and boards, pucks flying at high speed (over 160 kilometers per hour (100 mph) at times), and other players maneuvering (and often intentionally colliding, also known as "checking") pose a multitude of inherent safety hazards. Besides ice skates and sticks, hockey players are usually equipped with an array of safety gear to lessen their risk of serious injury. This usually includes a helmet, shoulder pads, elbow pads, mouth guard, protective gloves, heavily padded shorts, a 'jock' athletic protector, shin pads/chest protector and a neck guard. Goaltenders wear masks and much bulkier, specialized equipment designed to protect them from many direct hits from the puck.

The hockey skate is usually made of a thick layer of leather or nylon to protect the feet and lower legs of the player from injury. Its blade is rounded on both ends to allow for easy maneuvering.

Goaltenders' skates, however, have blades that are lower to the ice and more square than round; this is advantageous to the goalies, for whom lateral mobility and stability are more important than quick turns and speed.

History

The first skates had simpled metal blades tied to regular shoes. The sticks were thin pieces of wood until the 1930's. In 1897, G.H. Merritt introduced simple goalie pads by wearing the wicket-keeper's pads. All players played in simple leather gloves, until a Detroit goalie introduced the trapper and blocker in 1948, by experimenting with a of rectangular leather, and a baseball catcher's glove. Jacques Plante was the first regular user of the goalie mask; Clint Benedict used a crude leather version in 1928 to protect a broken nose.

The goalie mask evolved to Vladislav Tretiak design, the first helmet and cage combo. Considered primitive by today's standard, that sort of mask is only used by Chris Osgood. The other helmet and cage combo, used today only by Dominik Hasek and Dan Cloutier is often questioned, citing safety concerns. The most recognized goalie mask today resembles a highly fortified motorcycle helmet with a cage attached. The composite hockey stick era is very new. Tom Barrasso, when the Penguins won the Cup, was still using a wood stick.

General Equipment

Two things that are general, non-protective equipment are the hockey puck and the hockey sweater. On top of the protective gear, players wear a jersey or sweater which displays the team's logo or crest and colours, as well as the player's name and number.

Goaltending Equipment

— Goal stick

— Goal skates

— Goalie mask or helmet and wire facemask
— Chest and arm protector
— locker, worn on the hand that holds the stick
— Catch glove, worn on the opposite hand
— Goal jock or jill
— Goal pants, which are typically more protective than players pants
— Goal pads,up to knees
— Socks, covering the leg from the foot to just above the knee or above

Equipment Brands

Some of the leading manufacturers of hockey equipment are:

— Nike Bauer
— Reebok
— CCM
— Easton
— TPS
— Vaughn
— Sherwood
— Eagle
— Graf

Certification of Hockey Equipment

Many leagues require players to wear equipment, especially head and face protection, certified by trusted agencies. As of 2005, there are four groups that specify standards for hockey head and face protection:

— European Committee for Standardization (CEN)

— International Organization for Standardization (ISO)

— Canadian Standards Association (CSA)

— ASTM International

Most countries requires youth players to wear helmets and facemasks certified by the Hockey Equipment Certification Council (HECC). This group certifies equipment based on the ASTM standards; it does not write standards.

Facemask Controversy

Youth and college hockey players are required to wear a mask made from metal wire or transparent plastic attached to their helmet that protects their face during play. Professional and adult players may instead wear a visor that protects only their eyes, or no mask at all; however, some provincial and state legislation require full facial protection at all non-professional levels. Rules regarding visors and face masks are mildly controversial at professional levels. Some players feel that they interfere with their vision or breathing, or encourage carrying of the stick up high in a reckless manner, while others believe that they are a necessary safety precaution.

In fact, the adoption of safety equipment has been a gradual one at the North American professional level, where even helmets were not mandatory until the 1980s. The famous goalie, Jacques Plante, had to suffer a hard blow to the face with a flying puck in 1959 before he could persuade his coach to allow him to wear a protective goalie mask in play.

While the general characteristics of the game are the same wherever it is played, the exact rules depend on the particular code of play being used. The two most important codes are those of the International Ice Hockey Federation (IIHF) and of the North American National

Hockey League (NHL). North American amateur hockey codes, such as those of Hockey Canada and USA Hockey, tend to be a hybrid of the NHL and IIHF codes, while professional rules generally follow those of the NHL.

Ice hockey is played on a hockey rink. During normal play, there are six players per side on the ice at any time, each of whom is on ice skates. There are five players and one goaltender per side. The objective of the game is to score goals by shooting a hard vulcanized rubber disc, the puck, into the opponent's goal net, which is placed at the opposite end of the rink. The players may control the puck using a long stick with a blade that is commonly curved at one end. Players may also redirect the puck with any part of their bodies, subject to certain restrictions. Players can angle their feet so the puck can redirect into the net, but there can be no kicking motion. Players may not intentionally bat the puck into the net with their hands.

Hockey is an "offside" game, meaning that forward passes are allowed, unlike in rugby. Before the 1930s hockey was an onside game, meaning that only backward passes were allowed. The period of the onside game was the golden age of stick-handling, which was of prime importance in moving the game forward. With the arrival of offside rules, the forward pass transformed hockey into a truly team sport, where individual heroics diminished in importance relative to team play, which could now be coordinated over the entire surface of the ice as opposed to merely rearward players.

The other five players are typically divided into three forwards and two defencemen. The forward positions consist of a center and two wingers: a left wing and a right wing. Forwards often play together as units or lines, with the same three forwards always playing together. The defencemen usually stay together as a pair, but may change less frequently than the forwards. A substitution of an entire unit at once is called a line change. Teams typically employ alternate sets of forward lines and defensive pairings when shorthanded or on a power play. Substitutions are permitted at any time during the course of the game, although during a stoppage of play the home team is permitted the final change. When players are substituted during play, it is called changing on the fly. A new NHL rule added in the 2005-2006 season prevents a team from changing their line after they ice the puck.

The boards surrounding the ice help keep the puck in play (they can also be used as tools to play the puck), and play often proceeds for minutes without interruption. When play is stopped, it is restarted with a faceoff. There are two major rules of play in ice hockey that limit the movement of the puck: offsides and icing.

Under IIHF rules, each team may carry a maximum of 20 players and two goaltenders on their roster. NHL rules restrict the total number of players per game to 18 plus two goaltenders.

Penalty of Ice Hockey

A penalty in ice hockey is a punishment for inappropriate behavior. A referee makes most penalty calls. A linesman may call only obvious technical infractions such as too many men on the ice. In the NHL, the linesman may call major intent-to-injure penalties that the referee may have missed. The statistic used to track penalties is called Penalties In Minutes (PIM)

During a penalty, the player who committed the infraction is sent to the penalty box. In most cases, the penalized team cannot replace that player and is thus shorthanded for the duration of the penalty. Normally, hockey teams have five skaters (excluding the goaltender), so if one penalty is called, play becomes five-on-four.

This is called a power play for the attackers and a penalty kill for the defenders. A team is far more likely to score on a power play than during normal play. During a power play, the defenders are allowed to ice the puck without a stoppage in play. If the penalized team is scored on during a minor penalty, the penalty immediately ends. If the penalty is a double minor and there is more than two minutes left, the penalty clock is set to two minutes; if there is less than two minutes left in the penalty, it is over when the team with the powerplay scores. If the penalty is a major, the advantage continues no matter how many goals are scored.

When a penalty is called on the team not in possession of the puck, play is not stopped until the penalized team gains control of the puck (or a goal is scored, or the team in possession commits an infraction or penalty). Thus, deliberately taking a penalty will not stop an offensive onslaught by the opposing team. During delayed penalties, the other team's goaltender will often leave the ice to add an extra attacker, since the opposition cannot propel the puck into the net in any way, although it is possible for the team in control of the puck to score on its own net.

When a goaltender draws a penalty (except for a game misconduct or match penalty), he does not go to the penalty box. His penalty is served by a player that was on the ice at the time of the infraction. A bench minor - a penalty assessed to the team as a whole or a team official - is also served by a player on the ice at the time of the infraction. The coach may choose which player he wishes to serve the penalty in either of these situations. The exceptions of the match or game misconduct penalties require the goaltender to leave the ice immediately. In such cases, a backup goaltender can be put in play, or any player can serve as the goaltender and is allowed to use the goaltender's equipment.

Kinds of penalties

Minor

Lasts for up to two minutes. If the opposing team scores on the power play, the minor penalty expires and the penalized player may return to the ice. In USA Hockey and IIHF rules, coincidental minor penalties (where a minor is called against a player of each team as the result of a single incident) do not result in both teams playing one man down and require them to stay in the box until the first stoppage after their penalties have expired. This is to prevent to people leaving the ice at the same time during play, which can result in collisions, interference, or additional penalties. However, in the NHL offsetting minors currently do result in a 4-on-4 situation.

In the past, this was under the ref's discretion if the referees felt that a penalty was committed by a player for the express purpose of creating a 4-on-4. In this case (the "Edmonton rule", named for the Edmonton Oilers who used 4-on-4 play with their superstar lineup to create an advantage), the referees had the option of allowing substitutions for the penalized players resulting in 5-on-5 play. This rule was taken off the books as of the NHL lockout as being unnecessary.

Bench Minor

Similar to a minor; these are generally called for violations of the rules by players or team officials not on the ice, or for technical violations related to players or officials coming on or off the ice (such as too many players on the ice or an illegal substitution). A bench minor requires the team to select a player from those legally on the ice at the time of the whistle to serve a minor penalty for his team. If a bench minor is called for a player leaving the box before his penalty has expired (this is common in amateur leagues where penalty box officials are rare; it is virtually unheard of in the NHL where they are mandated), the player leaving the box serves the additional time.

Double minor

Lasts for up to four minutes. Served as two consecutive minor penalties: If a power play goal is scored during the first two minutes, only the first minor expires-the player must serve the remaining minor penalty. A double minor is assessed to a player when their foul causes the victim injury (in practice, this is limited to injuries drawing blood) or if the penalized player is too vocal/animated in their objection to the call. Though not part of official USA Hockey rules as of 2005-2006, some "in-house" amateur or non-checking leagues instruct referees to call a double minor for stick penalties such as high-sticking, slashing, tripping with the stick, hooking or cross-checking, regardless of whether an injury was sustained as a result.

Major

Lasts for five minutes. The penalized player must serve the entire penalty regardless of whether or not the opposing team scores on the power play. If a major penalty involves injury to the head or face, a fine may be assessed. Three major penalties in one game results in an automatic game misconduct penalty. In the case of simultaneous major penalties to each team (e.g., fighting), the penalties do not cause either team to play shorthanded. Fighting is the most common call for a major penalty, though a major can be given for flagrant or openly deliberate rule infractions that would otherwise result in a lesser penalty, such as vicious slashes, cross-checks or trips.

Many penalties that warrant a major penalty often carry an automatic game misconduct penalty, regardless of how many major penalties that player has accumulated in the game. It is rare to see a major penalty (besides fighting) assesed to a player which does not carry an automatic game misconduct penalty.

Misconduct

Lasts for ten minutes. This is a penalty to the player only; his team is not shorthanded during a misconduct (unless additional penalties are assessed). After the penalty expires, the penalized player must remain in the penalty box until the next stoppage of play. In the event that the time remaining in the period/game is less than that of the penalty, the player is usually sent to the locker room, as it would not be possible for him to continue playing unless the game was tied late in the final period, in which case the possibility of overtime could allow the player to continue playing. The player also is assessed a fine.

Game misconduct

The player is ejected from the game. This is a penalty to the player only; his team is not shorthanded (unless additional penalties are assessed). It also carries a fine. Some leagues also impose a game misconduuct to any player who is assessed three minor penalties, three major penalties, or a combination of any three minors/majors, depending on the league.

Gross misconduct

Similar to a game misconduct, except it implies an action of extreme unsportsmanlike conduct (such as abuse of officials or spectators) and can be assessed to any team official in addition to a player. It is defined as a travesty to the game. (Other examples include playing under the influence of alcohol or marijuana.) On June 20, 2007, the NHL voted to eliminate the term "gross misconduct" from its rulebook. The infractions that were listed under this term are now just referred to as game misconduct penalties. The most likely reason for the change seems to be the seldom use of the term (no penalty assesed by the NHL since 2000 has been classified as a gross misconduct). In fact, the term is rarely, if ever, used in any North American professional hockey league.

Match

The player is ejected from the game and is ordered to the dressing room immediately, and automatically suspended from the league until a hearing is conducted. There are two types of match penalties: a ten minute penalty for deliberate injury to an opponent and a five minute penalty for intent to injure. In each case, 10 minutes is assessed in the player's penalty records. Another player on the offending team serves the penalty for its duration and does not return to the ice until the entire penalty time expires.

Game disqualification (NCAA only)

Similar to a match penalty, except a player serves an automatic suspension equaling one game for each game disqualification penalty called against that player in a season (e.g., a two-game suspension for the second game disqualification of a season).

A player is given an attempt to score a goal without opposition from any defending players except the goaltender. This penalty is called for fouling an opponent from behind (not from a side swipe) when the player has no one but the goaltender to beat, or for any defending player including the goaltender who throws his stick in the defending zone. A penalty shot may also be called if a defending player other than the goaltender gathers the puck into his body or grabs the puck in the defending zone (handling the puck with the hands). A penalty shot is also awarded in the Southern Professional Hockey League in lieu of a power play during the final two minutes of an overtime for a minor penalty.

By far, minor penalties are the most common. Common minor penalties are for hooking, tripping, slashing, interference, cross-checking or roughing. Double minors tend to be a foul that would normally draw a minor penalty but also draws blood from the afflicted player, although others exist, most commonly a minor given for dissenting with an original penalty call.

Major penalties are assessed for infractions that could result in serious injury such as boarding and fighting, as well as flagrant or personally-motivated actions that would otherwise be a minor. Misconducts and game misconducts are given when injury results, there is the potential for one, or for persisting in the verbal abuse of a player, coach, or official. Match penalties are given for deliberate injury and attempted injury and serious disrespect of game officials, such as a coach refusing to let his team play a game or physically abusing an official.

For especially egregious infractions, a player will be suspended for a fixed number of games. In professional leagues, the player does not collect his salary during the suspension. Suspensions are not assessed during a game (except in the case of a match penalty), but decided in a hearing of league officials.

For infractions that are too minor to deserve a penalty such as icing, hand passes, and offsides, the team is penalized by a faceoff closer to their end, but this is not a penalty under the rules of hockey.

Coincidental penalties

When a team is shorthanded because of a penalty, upon its expiration the penalized player returns to the ice immediately and can join the play in progress. For penalties where a player must go to the penalty box but the team does not play shorthanded, the player must remain there after the penalty until there is a stoppage in play for some reason.

When both teams incur a penalty of the same type (for example, two minor penalties) during the same stoppage of play, they are said to be coincidental. In most leagues, coincidental penalties do not cause a team to be shorthanded; the penalized players must sit in the penalty box, but the teams remain at the same on-ice strength.

In the NHL and U.S. college hockey, when the teams are at full strength and coincidental minors occur, both teams must play one man down: play is four-on-four. If coincidental minors occur when either team is already shorthanded, the teams remain at the same numerical strength. When coincidental majors, such as those for fighting, occur, the teams stay at full strength.

Coincidental penalties are determined by time alone, not by the individual penalties. For example, if during a stoppage of play, one player is assessed a double minor penalty and two players from the other team are assessed minor penalties, those penalties are considered coincidental and play remains at five-on-five.

Teams must have at least three skaters on the ice. If a team that already is down to three men is penalized, that penalty does not start until one of the previous penalties expires. In this situation, the newly penalized player must sit in the box right away. When the original penalty expires, that player may not return to the ice until a stoppage of play, so that his team still has the correct number of players on the ice.

Minor penalties only expire when a team is shorthanded. If play is five-on-five, four-on-four, or three-on-three and a goal is scored, no penalties expire. In leagues which play with a four-on-four overtime, the first minor penalty means the offended team plays down one man; a second penalty while the first penalty is occurring means the team with the two-man advantage will actually add a player, making the penalty five-on-three until the next stoppage of play after the penalty expires.

In the Southern Professional Hockey League, with a three-on-three overtime, each minor penalty means the team with the power play will play with an additional skater during the first three minutes of the overtime. In the final two minutes, no power play is awarded; instead, officials award a penalty shot to the team which would have received the power play, mainly to give the team a better chance at winning the game, since a power play would not be fully awarded.

List of penalties

In the NHL, infractions that result in penalties include:

Abuse of officials: Arguing with, insulting, using obscene gestures or language directed at or in reference to, or deliberately making violent contact with any on or off-ice official. This generally is issued in addition to other penalties or as a bench penalty against a coach or off-ice player, and is grounds for ejection under a game misconduct or match penalty in most leagues including the NHL.

Aggressor penalty: Assessed to the player involved in a fight who was the more aggressive during the fight. This is independent of the instigator penalty, but both are usually not assessed to the same player (in that case the player's penalty for fighting is usually escalated to deliberate injury of opponents, which carries a match penalty).

Attempt to injure : Deliberately trying to harm an opponent (and/or succeeding). This type of infraction carries an automatic match penalty.

Boarding: Pushing an opponent violently into the boards.

Butt-ending (or Stabbing) : Jabbing an opponent with the end of the shaft of the stick. It carries an automatic major penalty and game misconduct.

Charging: Taking more than three strides and/or jumping before hitting an opponent.

Checking from behind : Hitting an opponent from behind is a penalty. It carries an automatic minor penalty and misconduct, or a major penalty and game misconduct if it results in injury. See checking.

Clipping: Delivering a check below the knees of an opponent. If injury results, a major penalty and a game misconduct will result.

Cross-checking: Hitting an opponent with the stick when it is held with two hands and no part of the stick is on the ice.

Delay of game: Deliberately stalling the game (for example, deliberately shooting the puck out of play, holding the puck in the hand, refusing to send players out for a faceoff, or even repeated deliberate offsides). As part of the rule changes following the 2004-05 NHL lockout, NHL officials also call an automatic delay of game penalty to goaltenders that go into the corners behind the goal line (outside a trapezoid-shaped area just behind the net) to play the puck. Some delay of game offenses, such as taking too long to send players to take a faceoff, are not punished with a penalty: instead, the official may choose to eject the center of the offending team and order him replaced with another player already on the ice.

Diving: Falling to the ice in an attempt to draw a penalty. Usually classified under "unsportsmanlike conduct" and only a penalty in the NHL.

Elbowing: Hitting an opponent with the elbow.

Fighting (Fisticuffs) : Engaging in a physical altercation with an opposing player, usually involving the throwing of punches or worse. Minor altercations such as simple pushing and shoving are generally called as Roughing.

Goaltender Interference: Physically impeding or checking the goalie. Visually impeding the goalie's view of the play with your body, called "screening", is legal.

Head-butting: Hitting an opponent with the head. A match penalty is called for doing so.

Touching an opponent with the stick above shoulder level. A minor penalty is assesed to the player, unless blood is drawn by the player hit by the stick. In this case, an automatic double-minor (4 minutes) is called. A penalty is not called when the puck is hit by a high stick, but play will be stopped and the ensuing faceoff will take place at a spot which gives the non-offending team an advantage. Also, a goal that is scored by means of high sticking will not be counted.

Holding: Grabbing an opponent's body, equipment or clothing with the hands or stick. Generally a minor; USA Hockey rules call for a major and a game misconduct for grabbing and holding a facemask or visor.

Holding the stick: Grabbing and holding an opponent's stick, also called whan a player deliberately wrenches a stick from the hands of an opposing player or forces him to drop it by any means that is not any other penalty such as Slashing.

Hooking: Using a stick as a hook to slow an opponent, no contact is required under new standards.

Illegal Equipment: Using equipment that does not meet regulations, either by size (length, width) or number (two sticks) or other guidelines (e.g. a goalie's facemask can no longer be the "Jason"-style form-fit mask, a player may not have a stick with a curve exceeding 3/4", nor may they play with a goalie's stick). If a player broke his stick, it is mandatory to drop the stick immediately and play without it until getting a replacement from the bench. Otherwise this penalty will be assessed to the offending player (some game summaries call this "playing with a broken stick").

In addition, in the NHL a player may not pick a stick up off the ground after it has been dropped (they can only receive a stick from another player or from the bench; goalkeepers may not go to the bench but must have a stick carried out to them). This rule is generally not enforced in amateur leagues except for broken sticks or egregiously out-of-spec equipment as the cost of acquiring gear that meets NHL specifications "post-lockout" is prohibitive, especially for goalies. However, as of 2009 USA Hockey will enforce the NHL goal equipment specs, as will IIHF. While allowing "big pads" until them, USA Hockey stated in their 2007 Official Rules and Casebook of Ice Hockey that they "strongly encourage" goaltenders to follow the new regulations before they take effect.

Instigator penalty

Being the obvious instigator in a fight. Called in addition to the five minute major for fighting.

Interference: Impeding an opponent who does not have the puck, or impeding any player from the bench.

Joining a fight: Also called the "3rd man in" rule, the first person who was not part of a fight when it broke out but participates in said fight once it has started for any reason (even to pull the players apart) is charged with an automatic game misconduct in addition to any other penalties they receive for fighting.

Kicking: Kicking an opponent with the skate or skate blade. Kicking carries a match penalty if done with intent to injure, but otherwise carries a major penalty and a game misconduct.

Kneeing: Hitting an opponent with the knee.

Roughing: Pushing and shoving or throwing punches that are not severe enough to be considered fighting. Also called in non-checking leagues when an illegal body check is made.

Slashing: Swinging a stick at an opponent, no contact is required under new standards.

Slew Footing: Rarely called, as it is easily concealed. Tripping an opponent by using your feet. Most of the time simply called as "Tripping"; Slew footing as a penalty in fact does not exist in the USA Hockey rulebook as of 2005-2006.

Spearing: Stabbing an opponent with the stick blade. It carries an automatic major penalty and game misconduct.

Starting the wrong lineup: This very rare bench minor penalty is called when the offending team fails to put the starting lineup on the ice at the beginning of each period, the exception being injuries. For this penalty to be called, the captain of the non-offending team must bring this breach of the rules to the referee's attention immediately at the first stoppage of play. Also the penalty may be given if a player is not put on the scoresheet at the beginning of the game and plays. The only way for this to be called is if the official scorer notifies the referee of this oversight.

Substitution infraction (Illegal Substitution)

This rare bench minor penalty is called when a substitution or addition is attempted during a stoppage of play after the linesmen have signalled no more substitutions (once the face-off is set) or if a team pulls its goalie and then attempts to have the goalie re-enter play at any time other than during a stoppage of play. Too many men on the ice and/or starting the wrong lineup can also simply be called a substitution infraction.

Too many men on the ice

Having more than six players (including the goalie) on the ice involved in the play at any given time. "Involved in the play" is key; players that are entering the ice as substitutes for players coming off may enter the ice once the player returning to the bench is less than eight feet from his team's bench; at that point the returning player is considered out of the play, even if the play passes in front of the bench, unless he actively makes a move for the puck. The player entering the ice is part of the play as soon as his skates touch the ice.

Unsportsmanlike conduct

Arguing with a referee; using slurs against an opponent or teammate; playing with illegal equipment; making obscene gestures or abusing an official. Can carry either a minor, misconduct, game misconduct or match penalty, depending on the gravity of the infraction (for instance, using obscene language to a referee initially results in a minor, but making an obscene gesture to an opponent, fan or official carries a game misconduct.) Also, in some leagues the penalty progression is different for players and team officials (for example, in the USA Hockey rulebook players get a minor for their first infraction, a misconduct for their second and a game misconduct for their third, whereas the option of a misconduct is removed for coaches; in addition, after each penalty for a team official, the penalty count resets itself).

Unsportsmanlike conduct may also be called if a player drops his gloves and stick in preparation for a fight, but the non-offending player does not drop his equipment and has committed no action (verbal or physical harassment) to attempt to instigate a fight.

Other leagues typically assess penalties for additional infractions. For example, most adult social leagues and women's hockey leagues ban all body checking (a penalty for roughing or illegal check is called), and in most amateur leagues, any head contact whatsoever results in a penalty.

Penalty as strategy

Coaches or players may occasionally opt to inflict a penalty on purpose, especially when they are trailing. In some cases, it is hoped that the infraction can be concealed from the officials, thereby not being called. Gordie Howe was one player renowned for his ability to inflict penalties without being called.

Hockey players that opt to inflict a penalty despite the punishment do so in order to degrade the opposing team's morale or momentum, or boost their own. This is most obvious in a hockey fight, but can arise from virtually any minor penalty. It is hoped that the temporary setback of a penalty kill will be offset by the effect on the two teams' overall play.

Hockey players also sometimes commit penalties with the intention of drawing the other player into a coincidental penalty, say for roughing. In many leagues including USA Hockey-governed amateur leagues but not in the NHL, coincidental minor penalties do not terminate until the first stoppage of play AFTER the penalties terminate. If a star player on the opposing team is sent to the penalty box and the team intentionally drawing the coincidental penalty can avoid a stoppage of play beyond two minutes, their opponents' advantage is diminished for the length of time that play continues uninterrupted. Similarly, coincidental major penalties for fighting terminate at the first stoppage of play also; NHL players will draw opponents into a fight with the object of having a star opposing player sit in the box for more than five minutes.

Another common reason to inflict a penalty on purpose is to rob an opposing player of an excellent scoring opportunity. In these cases a player may hold, hook, or impede another player who otherwise would likely have scored-preferring to kill a minor penalty than give up a likely goal. The overuse of such penalties is mitigated by the possibility of a penalty shot being called; however in some situations a penalty shot is preferable to the situation that was interrupted (such as a two-man breakaway).

When a penalty is taken for one of these reasons, it is commonly (yet informally) known as a good penalty. Hockey players known as "Pests" specialize their game in the strategy of trying to draw opponents into taking a penalty.

Rarely, penalties are also taken if a team is ahead by only a few goals late in the game. This should only be used if the winning team has an excellent penalty kill and the opposite team doesn't have a good power play. As they are down one man, it allows the winning team to ice the puck without consequence and kill off more time.

NHL penalty records

The record for the most penalty minutes in one season is

held by Dave Schultz of the Philadelphia Flyers with 472 in the 1974-75 NHL season. The record for most penalty minutes in a career is held by Tiger Williams who had 3966 over 14 years. The active penalty minute leader is Chris Chelios from the Detroit Red Wings, who has accumulated 2,803 PIM over 23 years.

The most penalties in a single game occurred in a fight-filled match between the Ottawa Senators and Philadelphia Flyers on March 5, 2004 when 419 penalty minutes were handed out. Statistically, a game misconduct counts as 10 penalty minutes, in addition to other penalties handed out. In rare cases (as a result of multiple infractions, for instance the player participating in multiple fights), multiple game misconducts may be handed to a player - that is merely statistical, not (automatically) a multi-game suspension, although the league will often suspend the player in a subsequent decision.

Official Ice Hockey

Fighting is an established aspect of ice hockey in North America, with a long history involving many levels of amateur and professional play and including some notable individual fights. Although a definite source of criticism, it is a considerable draw for the sport, and some fans attend games primarily to see fights. Fighting is usually performed by one or more enforcers on a given hockey team and is governed by a complex system of unwritten rules that players, coaches, officials, and the media refer to as "the code".Some fights are spontaneous, while others are premeditated by the participants.

While officials tolerate fighting during hockey games, they impose a variety of penalties on players who engage in fights. Unique to North American professional team sport, the National Hockey League (NHL) and most minor professional leagues in North America do not eject players outright for fighting but major European and collegiate hockey leagues do. Therefore, the vast majority of fights occur in the NHL and other North American professional leagues.

Physical play in hockey, consisting of allowed techniques such as checking and disallowed techniques such as elbowing, high sticking, and cross-checking, is inextricably linked to fighting. Broadly speaking, fighting exists in organized ice hockey to help deter overly rough play, to allow teams to protect their star players, and to create a sense of solidarity among teammates. It is possible for players to become notable solely for their fighting ability. These players are known as "enforcers."

The debate over allowing fighting in ice hockey games is ongoing, with most players, administrators, and fans favoring condoned fisticuffs. Despite its potentially negative consequences, such as heavier enforcers (or "heavyweights") knocking each other out, administrators like NHL commissioner Gary Bettman are not considering eliminating fighting from the game, since most players consider it essential. Additionally, the majority of fans oppose eliminating fights from professional hockey games. However, considerable opposition to fighting exists and efforts to eliminate it continue.

History

Fighting has been a part of ice hockey since the sport's rise in popularity in 19th century Canada. There are a number of theories behind the integration of fighting into the game, the most common of which being that the relative lack of rules in the early history of hockey encouraged physical intimidation and control.The implementation of some features, such as the blue lines in

1918, actually encouraged fighting due to the increased level of physical play. Creation of the blue lines allowed forward passing, but only in the neutral zone. Therefore, puck handlers played at close quarters and were subject to a great deal of physical play. The emergence of enforcers, who protected the puck handlers and fought when necessary, followed shortly thereafter.

In 1922, the NHL introduced Rule 56 which formally regulated fighting, or "fisticuffs" as it was called in the official NHL rulebook. Rather than ejecting players from the game, as was the practice in amateur and collegiate hockey, players would be given a five-minute major penalty. Rule 56 and its language also filtered down to the minor professional and junior leagues in North America. Promoters such as Tex Rickard of Madison Square Garden, who also promoted boxing events, saw financial opportunities in hockey fights and devised marketing campaigns around the rivalries between various team enforcers.

In the current NHL rulebook, the archaic reference to 'fisticuffs' has been removed; fighting is now governed under Rule 47 in the NHL rulebook. Referees are given considerable latitude in determining what exactly constitutes a fight and what penalties are applicable to the participants. Significant modifications from the original rule involve penalties which can be assessed to a fight participant deemed to have instigated the fight and additional penalties resulting from instigating a fight while wearing a face-shield.

Though fighting was rarer from the 1920s through the early 1960s, it was more brutal than it is today. Star players were also known to fight for themselves since fewer professional teams existed and competition was fierce for roster spots. Therefore, enforcers did not typically make professional teams. However, with the

NHL expansion in the late 1960s and the emergence of skilled players like Wayne Gretzky, enforcers became more common. The average number of fights per game rose above 1.0 during the 1980s. Many teams signed enforcers such as Dave Semenko, Marty McSorley, and Stu Grimson to protect and fight for smaller offensive players such as Gretzky, Paul Kariya, and Teemu Selänne.

Since the 1970s, three rules have curtailed the number and scope of fights in the NHL. In 1977, the league created the "Third Man In" rule which attempts to eliminate the bench-clearing brawl by providing for the ejection of the first player that joins a fight already in progress. Another rule automatically suspends the first player from each team that leaves the bench to join a fight when it is not their shift. As of the 2006-07 season, the "Instigator" rule, which adds an additional two-minute minor penalty to the player who starts a fight, has contributed to the decline of fighting in the NHL. As of the 2006-07 season, the average is just over .61 fights per game.

Rules

Fighting is illegal in the NHL, the North American junior leagues, and other North American professional minor leagues, where a five-minute major penalty is given. What separates these leagues from other hockey leagues and nearly all other sports is that they do not eject players simply for participating in a fight. However, fighting is punishable by ejection in the Peewee, College and European leagues, Olympic competition, and in women's hockey at any level.

The rulebooks of the NHL and other professional leagues contain specific rules for fighting. These rules state that at the initiation of a fight, both players must drop their sticks so as not to use them as a weapon.

Players must also "drop" or shake off their protective gloves in order to fight bare-knuckled (essentially, "throwing down the gauntlet"), as the hard leather and plastic of hockey gloves would increase the effect of landed blows. Players must also heed a referee warning to end a fight once the opponents have been separated. Failure to adhere to any of these rules results in an immediate game misconduct penalty and the possibility of fines and suspension from future games.

In many leagues, referees will permit a fight between two players to run its course until one or both players end up on the ice. Referees will actively try to break up fights involving more than two participants or multiple fights.

North American professional leagues

In the NHL, American Hockey League, ECHL, CHL, International Hockey League, and other notable minor leagues, officials punish combatants with five-minute major penalties for fighting (hence the phrase "five for fighting"). A player is automatically ejected and suspended if the player tries to leave the bench to join a fight, and is also automatically ejected for using weapons of any kind (such as using a skate to kick an opponent, using a stick to hit an opponent, or wrapping tape around one's hands), as they can cause serious injury. A player who receives two instigator penalties or participates in three fights in a single game is also ejected automatically. Furthermore, his coach can be suspended up to ten games for allowing players to leave the bench to join a fight.

A player who commits three major penalties, including fighting, during a game is automatically ejected, suspended, and fined. A player ejected for three major penalties in a game, or for use of weapons, cannot be replaced for five minutes.

In 2003, the ECHL added an ejection, fine, and suspension of an additional game for any player charged as an instigator of a fight during the final five minutes of the third period or any overtime. The NHL and AHL adopted the rule in 2005-06, and the NHL includes a fine against the ejected player's head coach.

Olympic

In Division I & III NCAA hockey, the fighters are given a Game Disqualification, which is an ejection from the game and a suspension for as many games as the player has accrued Game Disqualifications during the course of a season. For example, if a player engages in a fight having already received a Game Disqualification earlier in the season, he is ejected from the game and then suspended for his team's next two games. This automatic suspension has made fighting in college hockey relatively rare.

Fighting is prohibited in Olympic ice hockey and in European professional hockey leagues. The international rules (by IIHF) specify in the rule 528 - Fisticuffs or Roughing the following penalties (among others):

— Match penalty (the player is ejected from the game and another player serves 5 minutes on the penalty bench) for a player who starts fisticuffs.

— Minor penalty (2 minutes) for a player who retaliates with a blow or attempted blow.

— Game misconduct penalty (ejection from the game) in addition to any other penalties for any player who is the first to intervene in a fight which is already in progress.

— Double minor penalty (4 minutes), major penalty + game misconduct penalty (5 minutes and ejection from the game), or match penalty (at the discretion of the referee) for a player who continues the fighting after being told by the referee or a linesman to stop.

— Misconduct penalty (cannot play for 10 minutes; the second misconduct penalty in one game means automatic ejection) for a player who intentionally takes off his gloves in a fight.

Enforcer Hockey

The role of "enforcer" on a hockey team is unofficial but crucial to the game. Enforcers occasionally play regular shifts like other players, but their primary role is deterring opposing players from rough play. Coaches often send enforcers out when opposing enforcers are on the ice or any time when it is necessary to check excessively physical play by the opposing team. Historical players who have made a name for themselves within the sport by frequently engaging in fights include Red Horner, Lou Fontinato, John Ferguson, Dave Schultz, and Tiger Williams; modern-day players include Tony Twist, Jody Shelley, Marty McSorley, Rob Ray, Tie Domi, Kelly Chase, Georges Laraque, Ken Baumgartner, Donald Brashear, Joe Kocur and Bob Probert. Enforcers, particularly those with questionable playing skills, can be colloquially referred to as goons.

Causes

There are many reasons for fights during a hockey game. Some reasons are related to game play, such as retaliation, momentum-building, intimidation, deterrence, attempting to draw "reaction penalties", and protecting star players. There are also some personal reasons such as retribution for past incidents, bad blood between players, and simple job security for enforcers.

Of the many reasons for fighting, the foremost is for retaliation. When players engage in play that members of the opposing team consider unscrupulous, a fight can ensue. On rare occasions, the fight may be between the assailant and the victim or between the assailant and an enforcer from the victim's team, but most of the time the fight is between any two opposing enforcers. Fights that occur for retaliation purposes can be in immediate response to an on-ice incident, to incidents from earlier in the game, or to actions from past games. Enforcers who intend to start a fight have to consider their timing due to the Instigator rule. For example, putting the opposing team on a power play due to penalties incurred from fighting is less advisable when the game is close.

Enforcers sometimes start fights to build game momentum and provide a psychological advantage over the opposing team. These fights usually involve two enforcers, but may involve any player who is agitating the opposition. This type of fight raises morale on the team of the player who wins, and often gets the home crowd into the game as well. For that reason, it can also be a gamble to start a fight for momentum; if an enforcer loses the fight, the momentum can swing the wrong way.

Intimidation is an important element of a hockey game and some enforcers start fights just to intimidate opposing players in hopes that they will refrain from agitating skilled players. For example, in the late 1950s, Gordie Howe helped establish himself as an enforcer by defeating Lou Fontinato, a notable enforcer who tallied over 1,200 penalty minutes in his career. After that incident, Howe got a lot more space on the ice and was able to score many goals over the span of his career because he intimidated other players. Conversely, games in European professional leagues are known to be less violent than North American games because fighting is discouraged in Europe by ejection and heavy fines. Since the penalties for fighting are so severe, the enforcers are less able to intimidate opposing players with fighting and said players take more liberties on the ice.

For teams that face each other frequently, players may fight just to send the message to the opposing players that they will be the target of agitation or aggression in future games. Teams that are losing by a considerable margin often start these fights near the end of the game when they have nothing to lose. Enforcers may start fights with more skilled players to draw what is called a "reaction penalty", an undisciplined reaction to aggressive play on the part of the enforcer. This practice is also known to be difficult due to the Instigator rule.

Another reason is the protection of star players. Over the history of hockey, many enforcers have been signed simply to protect players like Gretzky, who was protected by Semenko, McSorley and others, and Brett Hull, who was protected by Chase and others. The NHL averaged twice as many fights during Gretzky's prime with the Edmonton Oilers than it did during the 1970s; some sources credit Gretzky with being a major cause in the statistical rise.

Personal reasons

Many young enforcers need to establish their role early in their career to avoid losing their jobs.[30] Due to the farm systems that most professional hockey leagues use, enforcers who get a chance to play at the level above their current one (for example, an American Hockey League player getting a chance to play in an NHL game) need to show other players, coaches, and fans that they are worthy of the enforcer role on the team.

There are also times when players and even entire teams carry on personal rivalries that have little to do with individual games; fights frequently occur for no other reason. An infamous rivalry that produced many fights was between the Detroit Red Wings and the Colorado Avalanche during the 1990s.

Efforts to ban fighting

Criticism of fighting in ice hockey typically arises after acts of violence committed during fights are singled out in the media. For example, on March 21, 2007, Colton Orr of the New York Rangers fought with Todd Fedoruk of the Philadelphia Flyers and ended up knocking him unconscious.

Fedoruk already had titanium plates in his face from a fight earlier in the season. The resulting media coverage of the incident renewed calls for a fighting ban. Some players acknowledge that there is no harm in discussing the issue; however, most players and administrators continue to insist that fighting stay as a permanent element of organized ice hockey. Some league administrators, such as NHL senior vice-president and director of hockey operations Colin Campbell, have been circulating and considering the idea of banning fighting in response to incidents such as the Fedoruk-Orr fight.

NHL perspective

"Fighting has always had a role in the game..from a player safety standpoint, what happens in fighting is something we need to look at just as we need to look at hits to the head. But we're not looking to have a debate on whether fighting is good or bad or should be part of the game."

Some sports journalists, mostly in Canada, have been articulating the idea with increasing frequency during the 2006-07 NHL season that fighting adds nothing to the sport and should be banned. Among the reasons they cite are that it is unsportsmanlike, is a "knee-jerk" reaction that detracts from the skillful aspects of the game, and that it is simply a waste of time. Opponents of fighting cite that international and college hockey, which both harshly penalize fighting with suspensions, lack the incidents or "stick work" violence proponents claim to fear, and question what it is about North American professional ice hockey players - unique to major professional team sport - that renders them incapable of controlling themselves on the ice without fighting.

Community members often become involved in the debate over banning fighting. In December 2006, a school board trustee in London, Ontario attended a London Knights game and was shocked by the fighting and by the crowd's positive reaction to it. This experience led him to organize an ongoing effort to ban fighting in the Ontario Hockey League, where the Knights compete, by attempting to gain the support of other school boards and by writing letters to OHL administrators. On the advice of its Medical Health Officer, the Middlesex-London Health board has supported recommendations to ban fighting across amateur hockey and to increase disciplinary measures to ensure deterrence.

There are several informal rules governing fighting in ice hockey that players rarely discuss but take quite seriously. The most important aspect of this etiquette is that opposing enforcers must agree to a fight, usually via a verbal or physical exchange on the ice. This agreement helps both players avoid being given an instigator penalty, and helps keep unwilling participants out of fights.

Enforcers typically only fight each other, with only the occasional spontaneous fight breaking out between one or two opponents who do not usually fight. Enforcers spend time researching the techniques and weaknesses of other enforcers, and many carry on long-standing rivalries. There is a high degree of respect among enforcers as well; they will respect a rival who declines a fight because he is playing with injuries, a frequent occurrence, because enforcers consider winning a fight with an injured opponent to be an empty victory. This is also known as granting a "free pass."

Long-standing rivalries result in numerous rematches, especially if one of the enforcers has to decline an invitation to fight during a given game. This is one of the reasons that enforcers may fight at the beginning of a game, when nothing obvious has happened to agitate the opponents. On the other hand, it is bad etiquette to try to initiate a fight with an enforcer who is near the end of his shift, since the more rested player will have an obvious advantage.

Another important aspect of etiquette is simply fighting fairly and cleanly. Fairness is maintained by not wearing equipment that could injure the opposing fighter, such as face shields, gloves, or masks, not pulling the opposing fighter's jersey over his head, and not assaulting referees or linesmen. Finally, whatever the outcome of the fight, etiquette dictates that players who choose to fight win and lose those fights gracefully. Otherwise, they risk losing the respect of their teammates and fans.

Tactics

Fighting tactics are governed by several actual rules, and enforcers also adopt informal tactics particular to their style and personality.

One tactic adopted by players is known as "going for it", in which the player puts his head down and just throws as many punches as he can, as fast as he can. In the process, that player takes as many punches as he delivers, although some of them are to the hard forehead. Fighters usually must keep one hand on their opponent's jersey since the ice surface makes maintaining balance very difficult. For this reason, the majority of a hockey fight consists of the players holding on with one hand and punching with the other. Enforcers such as Darren McCarty advocate letting the opposing enforcer get a few punches in before putting in maximum effort, and assert that fighting is as much about knowing how to take a punch as it is about delivering punches.

Other examples include Gordie Howe's tactic of holding the sweater of his opponent right around the armpit of his preferred punching arm so as to impede his movement. Probert, of the Detroit Red Wings and Chicago Blackhawks, was known to allow his opponents to punch until they showed signs of tiring, at which time he would take over and usually dominate the fight. Some consider long-time enforcer Rob Ray to be the reason that hockey jerseys are now equipped with tie-down straps that prevent their removal; he would always remove his jersey during fights so his opponents would have nothing to grab on to. This is commonly referred to as the "Rob Ray Rule".

Notable fights and brawls

Some fights have attracted significant media attention due to injuries sustained by one or both participants and other factors.

— Maurice "Rocket" Richard knocked out enforcer Bob Dill twice in one game. Dill had been hired by the New York Rangers specifically to rough up Richard.

— World Hockey Association Birmingham Bulls enforcer Dave Hanson, known for his 11-year professional career and role in the movie Slap Shot, fought hall of famer Bobby Hull of the Winnipeg Jets and in the process got Hull's wig caught in his knuckles. The incident landed Hanson in the news, and irate Winnipeg fans attempted to assault him on his way out of the arena.

— April 20, 1984 - A second-round playoffs matchup between the Quebec Nordiques and the Montreal Canadiens became a team melee at the end of the second period, after many smaller scaled battles had occurred throughout the game. The teams erupted into battle again before the third period began, provoked by the announcement of penalties and misconducts. A total of 250 penalty minutes and 10 game misconducts were handed out. This game prompted referee Bruce Hood to retire from the NHL once the playoffs ended.

— January 4, 1987 - A World Junior Ice Hockey Championships game between Canada and the Soviet Union was the scene of a bench-clearing brawl that lasted 20 minutes and prompted officials to turn off the arena lights in an attempt to stop it. The fighting was particularly dangerous as fighting was a surprise and a custom unknown to the Soviet players, some of whom escalated the fighting beyond what was considered acceptable in North America. The incident caused both teams to be ejected from the tournament, costing Canada an assured medal. A book by Gare Joyce was written regarding the event.

— March 26, 1997, Bloody Wednesday - The Avalanche and the Red Wings engaged in nine fights, including bouts between Darren McCarty and Claude Lemieux and goalies Patrick Roy and Mike Vernon. Lemieux, once ranked by ESPN as the NHL's most hated player, did not drop his gloves and instead bent down to his knees, and covered his head with his gloves to protect himself - a maneuver known as "turtling".

— March 5, 2004 - A Philadelphia Flyers - Ottawa Senators game resulted in five consecutive brawls in the closing minutes of the game, including fights between many players who are not known as enforcers and a fight between Flyers goalie Robert Esche and Senators goalie Patrick Lalime. The game ended with an NHL record 419 penalty minutes.

— February 22, 2007 - Every player on the ice in a Buffalo Sabres and Ottawa Senators game, including goalies Martin Biron and Ray Emery fought following an unpenalized hit and injury to Sabres captain Chris Drury. More than 100 penalty minutes were distributed Sabres coach Lindy Ruff was fined $10,000 by the NHL. He admitted to sending out a line of enforcers against Ottawa's skilled players and instructing them to "Go out and run 'em."

Notable promoters

— Fighting is a popular component of Don Cherry's Rock 'em Sock 'em Hockey video-highlight series. Cherry made 17 editions of the series which has sold more than a million videos.

— The Battle of the Hockey Enforcers involved Link Gaetz and featured just fights on ice but with no actual hockey played. The City of Prince George, British Columbia tried but failed to cancel the 2005 sporting event at the city-owned arena.

— In 2007, Derek Boogaard of the Minnesota Wild started hockey fighting camps for children, complete with T-shirts splattered with pretend blood. Boogaard argued that the focus was on teaching players how to protect themselves while critics argued that it contradicted efforts to renew youth interest in joining leagues.

In ice hockey, an official is a person who has some responsibility in enforcing the rules or maintaining the order of the game. There are two categories of officials, on-ice officials, who are the referees and linesmen that enforce the rules during game play, and off-ice officials, who have an administrative role rather than an enforcement role.

On-ice officials

As the name implies, on-ice officials do their job on the hockey rink. They are traditionally clad in a black hockey helmet, black trousers, a black-and-white striped shirt,and black polished skates with pure white laces. Thus, on-ice officials are often called zebras. They wear standard hockey skates and carry a fingerwhistle, which they use to stop play. They communicate with players, coaches, off-ice officials, and spectators both verbally and via hand signals. For many years (and currently in most minor and amateur leagues), officials had their last names on the back of their jerseys for identification, normally in a single row across the shoulders. (Some officials with long names would have their name in two rows.) Starting in 1996, however, NHL officials wear numbers on their shirts, a procedure adopted by other leagues.

A referee is responsible for the general supervision of the game. He can be identified by his red or orange armbands. His judgment of goals is final. He is the only official with the authority to assess penalties for violations of the rules.

Linesmen are primarily responsible for watching for violations involving the red line and the blue line. Such infractions include icing and offsides infractions. Linesmen also conduct faceoffs. They are also expected to break-up scuffles, and/or fistfights and other altercations that occur during the game. Some leagues allow linesmen to call penalties (such as too many men), while others only allow them to report the infraction to the referee.

In some leagues, such as the NCAA, the linesmen are given the title of assistant referee. When given this title, they are given more responsibility to stop play and call penalties that the referee may not see.

On-ice officiating systems

— The three-official system uses one referee and two linesmen. This is the most common officiating system. The NHL previously used this system until changing to the four-official system.

— The four-official system adds a second referee for a total of two referees and two linesmen. This system is used in the NHL and other high-levels.

— In the two-official system, each official acts as both referee and linesman-each has the responsibility to call both penalties and blue and red line violations. In this system, neither official wears red or orange armbands. This is used at lower levels of youth hockey and in most adult recreational leagues.

— In the 2-1 system, there are two referees and one linesman. There are a variety of ways to divide the responsibilities between the referees and linesmen. Typically, the back referee is responsible to make the initial call at the blue line when the puck first enters the zone, and after that the linesman takes over.

— The 1-1 system (sometimes called Texas two-man) uses one referee and one linesman. Often, this is an informal system used when one of the officials does not show up for a game scheduled to use the three-official system. The referee in this system must also make the occasional line call.

— The one-man system used in non-competitive

leagues. The referee makes all calls, though with less accuracy than in other systems.

Off-ice officials

Off-ice officials, with the exception of the video goal judge in professional leagues, do not have any direct impact on the outcome of the game. They serve primarily administrative and advisory roles.

The goal judge determines whether a player has scored a goal by watching to see if the puck has crossed the goal line completely. One goal judge is positioned outside the rink directly behind each goal net. For arenas so equipped, the goal judge turns on a red light behind the goal to alert everyone that a goal has just been scored. The red light (and the green light which is mounted next to it) are hooked up to the game clock: when the clock is stopped or the green light is turned on when the game clock reads :00, the red light cannot be turned on. The goal judge acts only in an advisory role; the referee has the sole authority to award goals and can override the opinion of the goal judge.

Video goal judge

The video goal judge reviews replays of disputed goals. As the referee does not have access to television monitors, the video goal judge's decision in disputed goals is taken as final. In the NHL, goals may only be reviewed in the following situations: puck crossing the goal line completely and before time expired, puck in the net prior to goal frame being dislodged, puck being directed into the net by hand or foot, puck deflected into the net off an official, and puck deflected into the goal by the high stick by an attacking player.

Official scorer

The official scorer keeps the official record of the game.

He is responsible for obtaining a list of eligible players from both teams prior to the start of the game. He awards points for goals and assists, and his decision in this regard is final. The official scorer typically sits in an elevated position away from the edge of the rink.

Penalty timekeeper

The penalty timekeeper records the penalties imposed by the referee. He is responsible for ensuring that the correct penalty times are posted on the score clock.

Game timekeeper

The game timekeeper is responsible for stopping and starting the game clock.

Statistician

The statistician records all required data concerning individual and team performances.

Like other "playing" sports, hockey game-play is based on referee decisions, therefore inevitable misunderstandings could seriously influence the whole process. And even if the mistake was committed purposely, there is no way that game results could be declared void because of it (the most probable outcome would be suspension or monetary penalty against the violating referee). Therefore, referees' influence in modern hockey culture is obvious.

Unlike hockey fans in other parts of the world, Russians have their own special name for on-ice officials: matras (Russian: ?????´c), which is Russian for mattress. In the Soviet era, mattresses were generally made with black-and-white stripes running down their length, reminiscent of the striped shirt of an official. Russian fans are so biased against the referees that even the most belligerent fans of opposing teams will support their counterparts in the face of questionable calls, regardless of whose team benefits.

Soviet hockey history with Moscow team domination started several myths, one of which is referees being corrupt (there are still rumours of Soviet leaders, like Stalin or Brezhnev, using phone calls to determine which team would win the game). While this fact is quite questionable, several standard practices serve only to help spread rumours. For example, league regulations state that referee's salary is paid by game hosting team and also that the largest punishment for a referee so far was a 3-month suspension with a questionable fine. Therefore, corruption is the main theme of Russian fans' performance. Most interesting cases include fans taking up 10 rouble note (a note with the lowest monetary value, typically equal to approx. 40 U.S. cents) from his wallet and addressing the referee with "A penalty, please" shout. When penalty is finally called (which takes no more than 5 minutes of normal gameplay), the note is thrown on ice, this time with "Thank you!" comment.

There are several popular chants to be heard on stands.

— Mat-ras - tri-dva-ras! (lit. "Mattress - three-two-one!") - "tri-dva-ras" is similar phonetically to pidorás, a derogatory term for passive homosexuals. Since swearing in public places is a civil offence in Russia, a workaround was found to avoid being captured by police.

— Sud'-ya - ka-zyol! (lit. "Referee(judge) is a goat!") - kazyol is a popular Russian pejorative.

— Sud'-ya - El-ton John! (lit. "Referee(judge) is Elton John!") - also casts illusions of sexual preferences.

— Po-lo-sa-tiy - pro-vo-ca-tor, hey-hey! (lit. "Striped is

an instigator, hey-hey!") - implies that referee is leading a game into an inevitable fight.

These pearls of Russian fan culture are characteristic not just for hooligans. Even serious businessmen in VIP lounges can be seen chanting some of these in extreme moments. A good example is a Metallurg Magnitogorsk vs. Dynamo Moscow game, which was broadcast live by the federal sports channel RTR Sport. During an overtime period, A Dynamo player managed to get a breakaway and shot the puck right into goalkeeper's face.

The latter fell, and a second shot of the former resulted in a goal. IIHF rules state that game stould be stopped immediately if a goalkeeper gets hit with the puck in his face so Metallurg officials appealed to the referee. After a video review, the appeal was denied resulting in huge "Matras - tri-dva-ras!" chant by each fan. Commentators even stopped their play-by-play, with a comment - "It seems, they're quite right". Cameras then showed VIP lounge with people chanting in similar manner.

Unfortunately, this examples show that ice hockey officials in Russia are treated quite poorly by fans. New insults are being constantly invented such as referees being called penguins. The league doesn't do anything to prevent this, in fact new league regulations (like a proposal to remove the referee's name from their jersey in favor of advertisements) have been criticised as bait for fan creativity.

Tactics

An important defensive tactic is checking - attempting to take the puck from an opponent or to remove the opponent from play. Forechecking is checking in the other team's zone; backchecking is checking while the other team is advancing down the ice toward one's own goal. These terms usually are applied to checking by forwards. Stick checking, sweep checking, and poke checking are legal uses of the stick to obtain possession of the puck. Body checking is using one's shoulder or hip to strike an opponent who has the puck or who is the last to have touched it (within a short period of time after possession; usually less than three seconds). Often the term checking is used to refer to body checking, with its true definition generally only propagated among fans of the game.

Offensive tactics include improving a team's position on the ice by advancing the puck out of one's zone towards the opponent's zone, progressively by gaining lines, first your own blue line, then the red line and finally the opponent's blue line. NHL rules instated for the 2006 season redefined icing to make the two-line pass legal; a player may pass the puck from behind his own blue line, past both that blue line and the center red line, to a player in front of the opponents' blue line. In fact, an errant pass that would normally result in an icing call is negated if the player for whom the pass was intended gains possession of the puck before it crosses the opponents' goal line; thus a "three-line pass" can be attempted with a fast forward as long as an off-sides is not committed. Offensive tactics are designed ultimately to score a goal by taking a shot. When a player purposely directs the puck towards the opponent's goal, he or she is said to shoot the puck.

A deflection is a shot which redirects a shot or a pass towards the goal from another player, by allowing the puck to strike the stick and carom towards the goal. A one-timer is a shot which is struck directly off a pass, without receiving the pass and shooting in two separate actions. A deke (short for decoy) is a feint with the body and/or stick to fool a defender or the goalie.

Headmanning the puck, also known as cherry-picking or breaking out, is the tactic of rapidly passing to the player farthest down the ice.

A team that is losing by one or two goals in the last few minutes of play will often elect to pull the goalie; that is, removing the goaltender and replacing him or her with an extra attacker on the ice in the hope of gaining enough advantage to score a goal. However, this tactic is extremely risky, and sometimes leads to the opposing team extending their lead by scoring a goal in the empty net.

A delayed penalty is a penalty offense committed by the team that does not have possession of the puck. In this circumstance the team with possession of the puck is allowed to complete the play; that is, play continues until a goal is scored, the puck is shot, stopped and controlled by the opposing goalie, a player on the opposing team gains control of the puck, or the team in possession commits an infraction or penalty of their own. Because the team on which the penalty was called cannot control the puck without stopping play, it is impossible for them to score a goal; in these cases the team in possession of the puck can pull the goalie for an extra attacker without fear of being scored on. This situation ends as soon as the team in possession completes the play and the penalty is assessed (if a delayed penalty is signalled and the team in possession scores, the penalty is still assessed to the offending player).

Although it is officially prohibited in the rules, at the professional level in North America fights are sometimes used to affect morale of the teams, with aggressors hoping to demoralize the opposing players while exciting their own, as well as settling personal scores. Both players in an altercation receive five-minute major penalties for fighting. The player deemed to be the "instigator" of an NHL fight, if one is determined to exist, is penalized an additional two minutes for instigating, plus a ten-minute misconduct penalty. If there is no instigator, both players stay in the penalty box for five minutes, and neither team lose skaters. This so-called instigator rule is highly controversial in NHL hockey: many coaches, sportswriters, players and fans feel it prevents players from effectively policing the objectionable behavior of their peers, which is often cleverly hidden from referees. [citation needed] They point to less extreme on-ice violence during the era before the rule was introduced. Toronto Maple Leafs owner Conn Smythe famously observed that "If you can't beat 'em in the alley you can't beat 'em on the ice."

The Neutral zone trap:

The trap is designed to isolate the puck carrier in the neutral zone preventing him from entering the offensive zone. In youth hockey development of the neutral zone trap often begins with the left wing lock. In this tactic the left wing plays in the normal position of the left defence men while in the offensive zone. The left defenceman then moves to the centre. The centre and right wing chase the puck. When the opposing team gains control of the puck, the defencemen and the left wing pull out and set a two man trap along the boards. The left or right wing available, backs up the trap while the centre and right wing pursuit and try to get in front of the play further blocking the offensive attack.

A game consists of three periods of twenty minutes each, the clock running only when the puck is in play. The teams change ends for the second period, again for the third period, and again at the start of each overtime played. Recreational leagues and children's leagues often play shorter games, generally with three shorter periods of play.

Various procedures are used if a game is tied. In tournament play, as well as in the NHL playoffs, North Americans favour sudden death overtime, in which the teams continue to play 20 minute periods until a goal is scored. Up until the 1999-2000 season regular season NHL games were settled with a single 5 minute sudden death period with 5 players (plus a goalie) per side, with the winner awarded 2 points in the standings and the loser 0 points. In the event of a tie (if the OT was scoreless), each team was awarded 1 point. From 1999-2000 until 2003-04 the National Hockey League decided ties by playing a single five-minute sudden death overtime period with each team having 4 players (plus a goalie) per side to "open-up" the game.

In the event of a tie, each team would still receive 1 point in the standings but in the event of a victory the winning team would be awarded 2 points in the standings and the losing team 1 point. The only exception to this rule is if a team opts to pull their goalie in exchange for an extra skater during overtime and is subsequently scored upon (an 'Empty Net' goal), in which case the losing team receives no points for the overtime loss. International play and several North American professional leagues, including the NHL (in the regular season), now use an overtime period followed by a penalty shootout. If the score remains tied after an extra overtime period, the subsequent shootout consists of three players from each team taking penalty shots.

After these six total shots, the team with the most goals is awarded the victory. If the score is still tied, the shootout then proceeds to a sudden death (actually sudden victory) format. Regardless of the number of goals scored during the shootout by either team, the final score recorded will award the winning team one more goal than the score at the end of regulation time. In the

NHL if a game is decided by a shootout the winning team is awarded 2 points in the standings and the losing team is awarded 1. Ties no longer occur in the NHL. Also, no statistics in the shootout count-no goals are awarded to players who score in the shootout, and goalkeepers are not credited with saves or goals against. Therefore, it is possible for a goalie to lose a game in which he gets a shutout. [citation needed]

Women's ice hockey

Lord Stanley of Preston's daughter, Lady Isobel Stanley, was a pioneer in the women's game and is one of the first females to be photographed using puck and stick (around 1890) on the natural ice rink at Rideau Hall in Ottawa. By the early 1900s, women's teams were common throughout most of the Canadian provinces, the long skirts they were still required to wear giving them a goal-tending advantage. On February 11, 1891, one of the earliest newspaper accounts of a game between women appeared in the Ottawa Citizen, and McGill University's women's hockey team debuted in 1894.

Ice hockey is one of the fastest growing women's sports in the world, with the number of participants increasing 400 percent in the last 10 years.While there are not as many organized leagues for women as there are for men, there exist leagues of all levels, including the National Women's Hockey League, Western Women's Hockey League, and various European leagues; as well as university teams, national and Olympic teams, and recreational teams. There have been nine IIHF World Women Championships.

Women's ice hockey was added as a medal sport at the 1998 Winter Olympics in Nagano, Japan. The United States won gold, Canada won silver and Finland won bronze.

The chief difference between women's and men's ice hockey is that bodychecking is not allowed in women's ice hockey. After the 1990 Women's World Championship, bodychecking was eliminated because female players in many countries do not have the size and mass seen in North American players. There are many who feel that the relative lack of physical play is a detriment to its popularity among the mainstream hockey public, while others feel its absence leads to a faster game more reliant on skating and puck-handling skills. [citation needed] In current IIHF women's competition, bodychecking is either a minor or major penalty, decided at the referee's discretion.

One woman, Manon Rhéaume, appeared as a goaltender for the Tampa Bay Lightning in preseason games against the St. Louis Blues and the Boston Bruins, and in 2003 Hayley Wickenheiser played with the Kirkkonummi Salamat in the Finnish men's Suomi-sarja league. Several women have competed in North American minor leagues, including goaltenders Charline Labonté, Kelly Dyer, Erin Whitten, Manon Rhéaume, and defenceman Angela Ruggiero.

Sledge hockey

Sledge hockey is a form of ice hockey designed for players with physical disabilities affecting their lower bodies. Players sit on double-bladed sledges and use two sticks; each stick has a blade at one end and small picks at the other. Players use the sticks to pass, stickhandle and shoot the puck, and to propel their sledges. The rules are very similar to IIHF ice hockey rules.

Canada is a recognized international leader in the development of the sport, and of equipment for players. Much of the equipment for the sport was first developed in Canada, such as sledge hockey sticks laminated with fiberglass, as well as aluminum shafts with hand carved insert blades and special aluminum sledges with regulation skate blades.

Pond hockey

Pond hockey is a form of ice hockey played generally as pick-up hockey on lakes and ponds. Pond hockey rules differ from traditional hockey, placing a greater emphasis on skating abilities.

The annual men's Ice Hockey World Championships are highly regarded by Europeans, but they are less important to North Americans because they coincide with the Stanley Cup playoffs. Consequently, Canada, the United States, and other countries with large numbers of NHL players have not always been able to field their best possible teams because many of their top players are playing for the Stanley Cup. Furthermore, for many years professionals were barred from play. Now that many Europeans play in the NHL, the world championships no longer represent all of the world's top players.

Hockey has been played at the Winter Olympics since 1924 (and at the summer games in 1920). Canada won six of the first seven gold medals. The United States won their first gold medal in 1960. The USSR won all but two Olympic ice hockey gold medals from 1956 to 1988 and won a final time as the Unified Team at the 1992 Albertville Olympics. Since all players in the communist system were "amateurs," the USSR's elite national team was the best the country had to offer, while the best Americans, Swedes, Finns, and Canadians were professionals and thus barred from Olympic competition. Nonetheless, U.S. amateur college players defeated the heavily favored Soviet squad on the way to winning the gold medal at the 1980 Lake Placid Olympics. This "Miracle on Ice" launched a surge of newfound popularity for a game about which many Americans had not cared much.

The 1972 Summit Series and 1974 Summit Series, established Canada and the USSR as a major international ice hockey rivalry. It was followed by five Canada Cup tournaments, where the best players from every hockey nation could play, and two exhibition series, the 1979 Challenge Cup and Rendez-vous '87 where the best players from the NHL played the USSR. The Canada Cup tournament later became the World Cup of Hockey, played in 1996 and 2004. The United States won in 1996 and Canada won in 2004. Since 1998, NHL professionals have played in the Olympics, giving the best players in the world more opportunities to face off.

There have been nine women's world championships, beginning in 1990. Women's hockey has been played at the Olympics since 1998. The 2006 Winter Olympic final between Canada and Sweden marked the first women's world championship or Olympic final that did not involve both Canada and the United States.

Culture of Ice Hockey

Like all of the major sports, hockey plays a major part in American popular culture. Though it is the least popular of the four professional sports in the US (American football, baseball, basketball, and hockey), a number of notable Hollywood films have been made about hockey. Notable hockey films include Slap Shot (1977), The Mighty Ducks (1992, successful enough to spawn two sequels and an NHL team named the Mighty Ducks of Anaheim; the team has since dropped the "Mighty" from their name to become the Anaheim Ducks), and Miracle (2004). The first two are fictional comedies; the last is a drama based on the true story of the 1980 "Miracle on Ice" USA Olympic gold medal team.

Other hockey films include Youngblood, Hockey Night, MVP: Most Valuable Primate, H-E Double Hockey Sticks, Mystery, Alaska, The Rocket: The Maurice Richard Story, The Sweater and the 1937 John Wayne film Idol of the Crowds . Many other films are less hockey-oriented but nonetheless prominently involve the sport. Both Happy Gilmore and The Cutting Edge centre around failed hockey players using their talents for other sports (golf and figure skating, respectively), while Wayne's World contains a number of prominent references to the sport during the film. The Jean-Claude Van Damme starrer Sudden Death (1995) is set and shot entirely in the Pittsburgh Civic Arena, the (supposed) stage for the seventh game of the NHL Stanley Cup finals.

While "National Lampoon's Christmas Vacation" was never a hockey movie, Chevy Chase's lead character, Clark Griswold, was famous for wearing a light Chicago Blackhawks jersey with "Griswold" and the numbers "00" on it during certain scenes. It also plays a part in Disney Channel original movies Go Figure and Genius, and romantic comedy Just Friends. In Quebec, the movie Les Boys is a cult classic for many hockey fans, enough to spawn 3 sequels. The fourth installment of Les Boys featured "Hockey Legends" such as Guy Lafleur, Pierre Bouchard, Martin Brodeur, Yvon Lambert and more.

Hockey also frequently shows up in American television, particularly in shows set in the colder regions of the US, such as the Northeast. One of the recurring characters on Cheers was Eddie LeBec, a French-Canadian Boston Bruins goalie who married regular character Carla Tortelli. LeBec later was cut from the team and joined a traveling ice show; the character was eventually killed off. One memorable episode of Seinfeld, "The Face Painter", involves the antics of Elaine's face-painting boyfriend Puddy, a rabid New Jersey Devils fan, and Jerry's stubborn refusal to thank an acquaintance for New York Rangers playoff tickets after the game when he had already thanked him numerous times beforehand. In NYPD Blue, the character of PA Donna Abandando, played by Gail O'Grady and a love interest of Detective Greg Medavoy in season 3, was a noted New York Rangers fan, having previously dated one of the players. Her Rangers pennant famously hung over her desk at the front of the squad room.

Many episodes of Home Improvement included references to the Detroit Red Wings and in one episode, Tim and his neighbour Wilson are at a game when Wilson wins the door prize. Actor Richard Dean Anderson has incorporated his personal love of hockey into two of his lead characters: MacGyver, and Stargate SG-1's Jack O'Neill. In an episode of The Simpsons, "Lisa on Ice", Bart is the star of his peewee hockey team, the Mighty Pigs, coached by Chief Wiggum. Lisa is eventually forced to become a goaltender on an opposing team-the Kwik-E-Mart Gougers, coached by Apu-to avoid a failing grade in gym, and she blossoms from a nervous wreck to an intimidating star. Eventually, the two teams play each other. Towards the end of the game, Bart is awarded a penalty shot, but before he shoots, he thinks of all his memories with Lisa. Lisa does this as well, and the two embrace each other. The finishes with the two teams tying each other and furious fans destroying the hockey arena.

In another episode, Bart answers his teacher's personal ad and uses the picture of hockey great Gordie Howe. More recently, the FX show Rescue Me, which stars Denis Leary, has featured hockey games as an integral part of several episodes; Hockey Hall of Famers and former Boston Bruins forwards Cam Neely and Phil Esposito have had cameos. Leary's character plays in the

FDNY vs. NYPD hockey game. Many Friends episodes also involve Joey, Chandler, and Ross attending New York Rangers games. At the end of one episode of Who's the Boss?, Tony and Angela are at a hockey game. Angela asks Tony what the red circle on the ice is for, and Tony indicates that it is blood (humorously furthering the stereotype of hockey violence). In Scrubs, Dr. Cox frequently wears a Detroit Red Wings jersey while not at the hospital; this is because of John C. McGinley's real-life friendship with Red Wings defenceman Chris Chelios.

Hockey has also been referenced many times in the series of six movies known as the View Askew Movies, which were written and directed by Actor/Director/Writer/Hockey Fan, Kevin Smith. His first movie, Clerks (1994), featured a street hockey game played on the roof of a store, however many of the players in the game wore ice hockey jerseys, including the New Jersey Devils, Pittsburgh Penguins, and a CCCP International Jersey. Mall Rats (1995) featured character Brodie (Jason Lee) playing an ice hockey game for Sega Genesis. Chasing Amy (1997) featured Joey Adams and Ben Afleck attending a high school ice hockey game. The other 3 movies, Dogma, Jay and Silent Bob Strike Back, and Clerks II didn't feature any ice hockey references, however Dogma did feature a street hockey reference.

Because of hockey's huge popularity in Canada, it is considered one of the most important elements of Canadian pop culture. It features often in homegrown television and movies, such as the CBC Television series Hockey: A People's History and Hockeyville, the Global TV reality show Making The Cut: Last Man Standing, as well as scripted shows like CTV's Power Play (1998-2000) and Showcase's Rent-A-Goalie (2006-).

Charles Schulz's beloved Snoopy is well known for his love of ice hockey. Snoopy's Home Ice (Redwood

Empire Ice Arena in Santa Rosa, CA) continues to host the annual Snoopy's Senior World Hockey Tournament each year.

Among the more famous hockey references in music is The Hockey Song by Canadian folk singer Stompin' Tom Connors. Warren Zevon is known for a hockey song called "Hit Somebody! (The Hockey Song)" from his 2002 album My Ride's Here. The song's title is in reference to the commonplace fights that tend to break out between players during games and tells the tale of Buddy, a Canadian farmboy turned hockey goon.

There are several less well-known songs which either directly or indirectly feature hockey references and hockey teams, such as "Zamboni" (a reference to the machine used to resurface the ice between periods and after games) by the Gear Daddies; "Helmethead" by Great Big Sea, which details the romantic exploits of an AHL player; and "Time to Go" by the Dropkick Murphys which references hockey directly, as well as the colours of Boston's NHL team, the Bruins (black and gold).

Canadian band The Tragically Hip has a number of songs that with hockey references, including "Fifty Mission Cap", about former Toronto Maple Leaf Bill Barilko, "Fireworks", and "Lonely End of the Rink". Their song "Wheat Kings" is not about hockey, but the Wheat Kings is the name of a hockey team in Brandon, Manitoba). In addition, "Heaven Is a Better Place Today" is a tribute to the late hockey player Dan Snyder.

Also, the American rock group Five for Fighting, whose name is a hockey penalty reference chosen by singer John Ondrasik, who is a major ice hockey fan. Also, L.A. hardcore band Donnybrook takes its name form a slang term referring to a fight between players during a hockey game.

The name of the Boston hardcore band Slapshot is an ice hockey reference, and they have taken this concept further with the album titles Sudden Death Overtime and Greatest Hits, Slashes and Crosschecks.

Attendance records

The largest hockey attendance in history was on October 6, 2001, for a game commonly known as the Cold War. Two college hockey rivals, University of Michigan and Michigan State University, opened their season with a game in Michigan State's outdoor football arena, Spartan Stadium. A $500,000 sheet of ice was used, and the temperature was 30°F. The game drew a record breaking 74,554 spectators, smashing the previous number of 55,000 attendance during the Sweden vs. Soviet Union game during the world championship in Moscow.

The largest crowd to ever watch an NHL game was during the Heritage Classic when 57,167 people watched the Edmonton Oilers battle the Montreal Canadiens. The game was held at Commonwealth Stadium in Edmonton, Alberta, on November 22, 2003. Montreal edged Edmonton 4-3. The unique thing about this game is that it was the only NHL game to be played outside. Another memorable thing about this game was Canadiens' goaltender José Théodore's toque, which he wore outside of his mask.

An old-timers game (referred to as the MegaStars game) was played prior to the NHL game and featured an alumni of Oilers playing against a squad of former Canadiens. This is the only alumni game in which Wayne Gretzky has played since retiring, and he maintains it will also be the last.

Hockey expressions

— Chirping - trash talking

— Mucking it up - popular term for getting physical on the ice, going into the corners after the puck

— Between the pipes or in the cell - a goal

— Up on the roof - a shot that comes high towards the goal

– Gong Show - one that is terrible at hockey

— Top Shelf/Drawer - A goal that enters the net in either of the top corners

— Bender - one who skates on the inside of his edge and ankle bends in.

— Duster - one who is on the team but never plays

— Grinder - a player who works hard and is physical

— Bush leaguer - anyone who doesn't play to his or her ability.

— Sieve - A goalie who has a large amount of goals scored against.

— Ankle Breaker - A move in which a forward forces a defense-man to trip over his own ankles.

7

Road Hockey

Road hockey, also known as street hockey, dek hockey, ground hockey, or ball hockey is a version of ice hockey (or inline hockey) played with or without skates. It is possible to play with either a puck or ball, although a roller hockey puck is required when not on ice. Generally, the game is played with little to no protective equipment, therefore intense physical contact is not very common and is played without body checking but does permit a level of physical contact similar to that allowed in basketball. Though, when playing among friends, it's not uncommon for a fight to break out. An ice hockey puck would only work on a frozen over street. If a puck is used, for safety the puck usually must not be raised in the air (lifted or roofed). However, rules and playing styles can differ from area to area depending upon the traditions a certain group has set aside.

On ice the game is played in boots; on pavement it may be played in shoes or in inline skates. The goals often are marked by whatever objects are handy (for example, using two soda cans or water bottles as goal posts), although goal nets either designed for street hockey or ice hockey could also be used.

Due to the general prohibition of body checks, most of the pads and other safety equipment used for ice or roller hockey are not worn or required to be worn in street hockey games. However, most "skaters" tend to play with a minimum of hockey gloves and shin guards. Shin guard are often of the soccer type when the game is played on foot. Goalies typically wear equipment similar in appearance to their ice hockey counterparts so as to help block more of the goal area. However, such goalie equipment used in street hockey is generally lighter than that used in ice hockey due to the reduced weight and density of the ball that is typically used in street hockey as compared to the rubber puck used in ice hockey.

A street hockey stick is a special kind of stick. It has two main parts, the shaft, or stick, and the blade. The shaft is often made of aluminum or wood. The blade is usually made of polyurethane, the same thing as skateboard wheels. The blade attaches to the shaft by a screw. Some street hockey sticks are made in one-piece form and are made out of plastic.

The word 'CAR!' is a common one to hear on busier streets which generally means 'stop the game and move the goal nets'. This is often followed by the phrase "game on" once the car has passed. The game often begins with a so called 'NHL faceoff', in which the two opposing centers hit their sticks against each other three times saying "N", "H", "L". Immediately following the "L" the two players fight to see who claims possession of the ball.

Although road or street hockey is popular throughout Canada and parts of the United States, some residents in Canada have been raising concerns about how road hockey disturbs the neighbourhoods with the noise that the game creates and balls being accidentally flicked into the residents' yards.

A popular alternative to playing hockey on the street in Canada is to play in outdoor lacrosse boxes. The lacrosse boxes contain the same asphalt surface as the streets, but offers a more realistic feeling of hockey since the playing area is larger than the average street, plus there are boards that surround the lacrosse box. The only downside to this is the smaller size of the lacrosse nets that are already in place.

Similarly to lacrosse boxes, outdoor roller hockey rinks are becoming quite popular in public areas around the United States which allow for a place to play off the sometimes dangerous streets. Outdoor roller hockey rinks are usually covered in a sport court surface so equipment does not wear down as quickly as on asphalt. Many can also be covered to allow play during wet weather, and lighted for nighttime hockey.

In the United States the term "street hockey" is a generic one and usually refers to an ice hockey based game that is played without inline skates (when inline skates are worn the game is usually called roller hockey) and is rarely played on public streets. In the United States "street hockey" is most often played on outdoor basketball or tennis courts as well as indoor basketball courts and/or gymnasiums. The walls or fencing of these "rinks" serve to keep the ball (or the less often used puck) in play similarly to the boards of an ice rink. The United States definition of "street hockey" is more closely related to that of the Canadian terms "dek hockey" or "ball hockey."

In 1970 Raymond W Leclerc regarded as the Founder and Father of organized Street Hockey/Dekhockey in the USA and Canada. Ray Leclerc created the NO BOUNCE ORANGE BALL.

Mr Leclerc then established the basics of the game an Official Rink 160 ft long by 80 ft wide, special lightweight protective equipment and a game that featured NO CHECKING and that all players ages 4 to over 50 could play. He then established an organisation

ASHI/IDTA with a special Street Hockey Rule Book to control the game. Mr Leclerc built a model site to play and advance the game known as "Home of Street Hockey" in Leominster Ma., 3 Outdoor rinks, with the Headquarters and governing body of Street Hockey/ Dekhockey. The next evolution took place with the first sanctioned Official US Nationals played in Leominster Ma in 1974.

Today the US Nationals are an annual event and the game has advanced with Indoor and Outdoor rinks playing on special plastic modular Sports Surface. Tournaments continue are all over the world and most recently in 2006 Disney World, Orlando, Florida hosted the first USA CUP.

There are now a number of organised street hockey/ dek hockey/ball hockey leagues throughout the United States and the world, in a number of cities, and for a variety of age groups. These leagues are played both indoors and outdoors, usually on rinks used by roller hockey leagues. Street/dek/ball hockey has a national organisation and world championships. One non-professional Canadian league is the Canadian Ball Hockey League in which teams from across Canada play in the U.S. under rules variant to standard Dek Hockey. There are also many regional hockey leagues throughout Canada including the York Central Ball Hockey League. Headquaretred in Toronto, Canada it administers leagues and tournaments for all levels of play from beginner to advanced.

Road Hockey in Pop Culture

In the Disney film D2: The Mighty Ducks, the team learns from a gang of street hockey players. Street sports are often known for their tricks, and this film popularised the knuckle puck shot.

In Wayne's World, the main characters play road hockey, and the custom of yelling "CAR!" and "GAME ON!" was illustrated by them. In Road Hockey Rumble two hosts spend each episode searching out the best teams they can to compete against each other at road hockey. In Clerks., the main characters close the store to play road hockey on the roof.

Nomenclature Road Hockey

— In Central Ontario, long considered a hockey hotbed, the term 'yard sale' refers to the dropping of player equipment and the beginning of a fight.

— "Goal suck," "loafer", "The Donsky" or "cherry picker" refers to players who stays in the opponent's end, waiting for an easy chance to score.

— "Hog" is often used as a term for a game of road hockey in which two teams shoot on one goalie.

8

Rollar Hockey

Roller Hockey (Quad) is highly popular and has many names worldwide that mean the same sport. Some common names for names Roller Hockey (quad) are: Hóquei em Patins, International Style Ball hockey, Rink Hockey or Hardball Hockey. Roller Hockey was a demonstration rollersport in the 1992 Barcelona summer Olympics. There have been many world championships, Latin countries dominating the sport since the 1940s: Portugal (15 World titles), Spain (13 World titles), Italy (4 World titles) and Argentina (4 World titles). Other countries, such as France, Brazil, Germany, Switzerland, Andorra and England are regular international competitors, but rarely overcome the traditional powers. Roller Hockey (Quad) is referred to as Hardball Hockey in the United States.

Roller Hockey is a very fast sport, which may create a problem for TV transmissions, and new rinks are built using blue or white pavement to make the ball more visible on TV. It was a demonstration sport in the 1992 Summer Olympics in Barcelona. The most important clubs in Europe (and, arguably, the world) are FC Porto, SL Benfica and Óquei de Barcelos from Portugal, FC Barcelona, Reus Deportiu, Igualada and Liceo de Coruña from Spain, and occasionally Primavera Prato, Follonica and Bassano Hockey 54 from Italy. In terms of trophies won FC Barcelona is the most successful team having won seventeen European Cups.

Every two years FIRS organises a Roller Hockey (Hardball hockey, Hoquei em Patins, Roller Hockey) and a Ladies Rink Hockey World Championship. A complete list of medal standings and where the World Championships were held can be found at Mens Roller Hockey World Championships and at Ladies Roller Hockey World Championships.

Game

Two five-man teams (four skaters and one goalkeeper) try to drive the ball with their sticks into the opponents' goal. The ball can only be put in motion by a stick. The game has two 25-minute halves (for adults), with the clock stopping when the ball becomes dead. Each team has a one-minute timeout in each half.

Rink

The rink has usually a polished wooden surface, but any flat, non-abrasive and non-slippery material such as treated cement is acceptable. Likewise, it is allowed for rink owners to put advertisements in the playing area, as long as they don't interfere with ball or skate motion, which includes both physically (must be at the exact same level as the remaining area) and visually (dark colours or any other pattern which can mask the ball).

It can have one out of three standard sizes (a minimum of 34x17 meters, an average of 40x20 and a maximum of 44x22) or any size between the minimum and maximum values that has a 2:1 size ratio with a 10% margin of error.

The rink has rounded corners (1 m radius) and is surrounded by a 1 m wall. The wall also has a wooden base 2 cm wide and at least 20 cm high. Behind the goals there is a 4 m high net, even if there are no stands (to avoid the ball bouncing back from a wall and hitting a player). If the ball hits the net, it's considered to be out of bounds.

The markings are simple. The halfway line divides the rink into halves, and 22 m from the end wall an "anti-play" line is painted. The area is a 9 X 5.40 m rectangle, placed from 2.7 to 3.3 m ahead of the end table. It has a protection area for goalkeepers, a half-circle with 1.5 m radius. All markings are 8 cm in width. The goal (painted in fluorescent orange) is 105 cm high by 170 cm wide. Inside the goal there is a thick net and a bar close to ground to trap the ball inside (before, two extra referees stayed behind the goal to judge goal decisions), and 92 cm deep. While not attached to the ground, it is extremely heavy to prevent movement.

Equipment

— The clothing is similar to that used in football (soccer)-socks up to the knee, shorts and a shirt.

— Sticks are different for skaters and goalkeepers. They can be of any material approved by the CIRH (although wooden sticks are still most often used), with a minimum length of 90 cm and maximum of 115 cm. They cannot be wider than 5 cm or weigh over 500 g.

— The ball is made of vulcanised rubber, has a 23 cm in circumference, and weighs 155 g.

— The skates must have two pairs of wheels, with a minimum diameter of 3 cm. Players are allowed to use brakes in the front of the skate, with a diameter or larger side not larger than 5 cm.

— Protective material includes shin guards, knee caps,

jock strap and gloves. Specifications for helmets and elbow caps vary from federation to federation.

– Goalkeepers (or netminders) use protective padding on the torso (plus shoulders) (the maximum amount is being regulated, since, as in ice hockey, many goalkeepers have been using massive protection to make them larger and broader), neck guard, large shin guards (not longer than 75 cm), gloves protecting the whole forearm and a helmet with either a grid or unbreakable transparent material. Unlike the Roller Hockey (Inline) Goalie who uses a Catch Glove to catch the shot on goal, the Roller hockey (Quad) Goalie uses a flat batting glove that provides rebound characteristics when blocking a shot on goal.

9

Unicycle

A unicycle is a one-wheeled human powered vehicle. Unicycles are similar to, but less complex than, bicycles. Unicycles are composed of a few key parts: the wheel (which includes the tire, tube, rim, spokes, hub and axle), the cranks, pedals, fork-style frame, seatpost, and saddle (the seat of the unicycle). The wheel is usually similar to a bicycle wheel with a special hub designed so the axle is a fixed part of the hub. This means the rotation of the cranks directly controls the rotation of the wheel (called direct drive). The frame sits on top of the axle bearings, while the cranks attach to the ends of the axle. The seatpost links the frame to the saddle.

There are many different types of unicycles, which can include (but are not limited to): freestyle unicycles, trial unicycles, MUnis, giraffes, and long distance unicycles, which all have special components unique to that type of unicycle.

History of Unicycle

The unicycle's history began with the invention of the bicycle. Comte De Sivrac first developed bicycles during the late eighteenth century. His device, called a celerifere, was a wooden horse that had two wheels joined by a wooden beam. Germany's Baron von Drais improved the design by adding a steering mechanism and introduce his Draisienne or Hobby Horse in 1818. Kirkpatrick Macmillan, a Scottish blacksmith, added cranks and pedals to the front wheel in 1839, and called it the Velocipede. The first mass-produced riding machine, the Michaux Velocipede, was designed in 1863. In 1866, James Stanley invented a unique bicycle called the Penny Farthing with a very large front wheel and a small rear wheel. It is this vehicle that is thought to be the inspiration for the unicycle.

One theory of the advent of the unicycle is based on the popularity of the penny farthing during the late nineteenth century. Since its pedal cranks were connected directly to the front axle, the rear wheel would go up in the air and the rider would be moved slightly forward. This likely prompted riders to see how long they could ride with the back wheel in the air and the unicycle was born. Evidence for this theory of development can be found in pictures from the late eighteenth century that show unicycles with large wheels.

Over the years, unicycle enthusiasts have inspired manufacturers to create new designs, such as seatless (the ultimate wheel) and tall (giraffe unicycle) unicycles. During the late 1980s some extreme sportsmen took an interest in the unicycle and off-road unicycling (MUni) was born.

Kinds of Unicycles

Freestyle Unicycle

Generally used for flatland skills and routines. Usually has a relatively high seatpost, a narrow saddle, a squared fork (used for one-footed tricks), and cotterless cranks, as they do not need to withstand too much pressure. These unicycles are used similarly to flatland bicycles. Some examples of a freestyle unicycle include: Miyata, Nimbus,

Schwinn, and Semcycle brands. Prices can range from less than $100 USD to over $300 USD. Wheel size is usually 20 inches, but smaller riders may use 16-inch unicycles. Some people prefer 24-inch wheels. A freestyle unicycle is stronger than most other types of unicycles.

Trials Unicycle

Designed for unicycle trials, trials unicycles are stronger than standard unicycles in order to withstand the stresses caused by jumping, dropping, and supporting the weight of the unicycle and rider on components such as the pedals and cranks. A recent development in trials unicycles is splined cranks, a feature that is very useful and somewhat expensive. Many trials unicycles also have wide, 19- or 20-inch, knobby tires to absorb some of the impact on drops. For more info, see the trials unicycle page.

Offroad Unicycles

MUni is the shortened phrase for mountain unicycling. Munis have many of the same components as trials unicycles, but have a few key differences. Usually, the tire diameters on mountain unicycles are either 24 or 26 in., allowing the rider to more easily roll over obstacles such as roots and rocks. The seat is also thicker and more comfortable on MUnis to compensate for the rough terrain. Brakes are sometimes used for steep descents. KH unicycles and Schlumpf Innovations are currently working together to make the world's first geared MUni.

Touring Unicycles

Used for long distances, these unicycles are specially made to cover distances. They have a large wheel diameter, between 26 and 36 in., so more distance is covered in less pedal rotation. A 36" unicycle made by the Coker company started the big wheel trend. Some variations on the traditional touring unicycle include the 'Schlumpf GUni' (geared unicycle), which uses a unique two-speed internal fixed-geared hub. Larger direct-drive wheels tend to have shorter cranks to allow for easier cadence and more speed. Geared wheels, with an effective diameter larger than the wheel itself, tend to use longer cranks for control, as the speed comes from the gear ratio not the wheel itself. Modern unicyclists routinely cover distances unheard of just a few decades ago.

Variations

— *Giraffe unicycle:* a tall unicycle, usually chain-driven (but includes Multi-wheel unicycles).

— *Geared unicycle (aka GUni):* a unicycle whose wheel rotates faster than the pedal cadence. Used for distance riding and racing.

— *Multi-wheeled unicycle:* A unicycle with more than 1 wheel, stacked on top of each other so only one touches the ground. The wheels are linked together by chains or direct contact with each other.

— *Kangaroo unicycle:* unicycle that has both the cranks facing in the same direction & the hub off-center. They are so-named due to the rising and falling motion of the rider supposedly resembling the jumping of a kangaroo.

— *Ultimate wheel:* a unicycle with no frame or seat, just a wheel and pedals.

— *BC wheel :* a wheel with pegs or metal plates connected to the axle for the rider to stand on. These wheels are for coasting and jumping. A purist form of unicycling. There are no cranks.

— *Monocycle (or monowheel):* a large wheel in which the rider sits inside (like a hamster wheel) and either pedals an internal drive or is motorized. It is not plagued by the normal unicycle balance problems because of the greater gyroscopic properties and lower center of mass.

— *Eunicycle:* a computer-controlled, motor driven, self-balancing unicycle.

— *Freewheeling unicycle:* a unicycle where the hub freewheels, allowing the rider to coast or move forward without pedalling, as a bike would. These unicycles almost 'always' have brakes because they cannot stop the way traditional unicycles do. These unicycles also cannot go backwards.

— *A quick list of other variations:* Tandem, Recumbent, Hydraulic Giraffe, Unibike, Suicycle, Motorized unicycle.

Theory

A unicycle is a form of inverted pendulum. It is also a nonholonomic system because its outcome is path-dependent. Balancing a robotic unicycle or a eunicycle forms an interesting problem in control theory.

Speed

The pedals of a typical unicycle (not a giraffe) are connected directly to the wheel. This means that there are no gears to shift like on a bicycle. It also means that wheel size is a major factor in unicycle speeds:

Wheel size	Avg	High
20"	3 mph	8 mph
24"	5 mph	10 mph
29"	7 mph	14 mph
36"	11 mph	22 mph

Riding

Traditionally, unicycling has been connected with

parades or the circus. This is because the unicycle requires a great degree of skill to ride, and many people who could ride them became entertainers. Recent developments in the strength and durability of bicycle (and consequently unicycle) parts have given rise to many riding styles such as trials unicycling and mountain unicycling. Unicycling has therefore developed from primarily an entertainment activity, to a competitive sport and recreational vehicle.

Riding styles

Neighborhood: For basic unicycling, this is the place to be. Not too long ago, all mass-produced unicycles were in this category. Basic, cheap unicycles such as the Torker CX are used.

Freestyle unicycling: Freestyle means to do skills, stunts, or tricks. Not only is freestyle a well-known term in BMX bicycling, it is also the name for a competition event in unicycling.

Trials unicycling: Trials unicycling is specifically aimed at hopping and riding over obstacles. Because of the constant pounding a trials unicycle endures, it must have a very strong axle and crankset.

Street unicycling: Street unicycling (or simply "street" as it's known within the sport) is a style of unicycling where riders use combinations of objects found in urbanized settings, such as curbs, ledges, handrails, stairs as well as flat areas to perform a wide variety of tricks.

Off-Road - Mountain Unicycling (MUni): Rough Terrain unicycling is attracting a lot of attention and has been the swiftest growing form of unicycling in recent years. Any place a mountain bike can go, a mountain unicycle can go as well (and sometimes better)

Touring or Commuting: This style is meant for distance riding. With a 29-inch or 36-inch wheel cruising speeds of 10 to 15 mph can easily be reached. However, the smallest wheel diameter to fit within the Touring category is 26 inches.

Racing: 100 meter, 400 meter, 1600 meter races and more.

Novelty: This category includes any unusual cycles not covered by our other categories. Examples include tall giraffe unicycles, multi-wheelers (wheels stacked), kangaroo and others.

Extreme Unicycling

Recently, unicycling has gained popularity as a sport, and as a general means of transport. In the last 10 years, unicyclists have taken unicycles out of the traditional parade, gym, or circus setting and have created new areas of unicycling. These areas can be described as:

Unicycle trials: Trials involves riding over obstacles of any sort, either in natural terrain or in an urban environment. The challenge relates to technical difficulty over short distances, and the objective is to use any riding techniques necessary to ride up, over, or down an obstacle without falling.

Mountain unicycling (Muni): Combines cross-country and trials challenges, where the objective is to ride technically difficult terrain over some distance. Extreme sport videos and films typically show Muni as primarily descents of difficult terrain, but the term also includes difficult uphill riding. The other purpose of this venture is to practice leaps using the wheel pressure to propel oneself up to a rock, or up a slope.

Flatland: The purpose of flatland (also known as freestyle) is to ride a unicycle in different ways, collectively referred to as "freestyle tricks". There are thousands of different ways to ride a unicycle, but the most popular tricks have been categorized in a skill measurement system called the "IUF Achievement Skill Levels". Flatland is typically done indoors in a gymnasium or outside on pavement where the terrain is smooth and predictable.

Street unicycling: Combines Trials and Freestyle techniques, and is typically done in urban areas. The objective is to perform freestyle tricks on obstacles. The overall difficulty relates not only to the difficulty of the obstacles but also to the difficulty of the tricks. This is different from pure trials because just riding over obstacles is not the ultimate objective; rather, the obstacles are used as props to set up the tricks.

[edit] Equipment / Safety

Wrist guards: The most common impact points when falling from a unicycle are the hands and wrists. Of all the safety gear, wrist guards receive the most wear and tear.

Knee and elbow pads: The second most common impact point are the knees followed by the elbows.

Helmet : A helmet is especially important with specialty riding like MUni.

Shin guards: Shin guards become a necessary piece of equipment when using metal or pinned pedals. These types of pedals grip the shoes better, but can cause injury to the legs.

Cycling shorts : Padded cycling shorts are designed with a seamless, padded crotch, and long enough legs to extend down past the saddle, making them much more comfortable than "normal" shorts.

Famous and Notable Unicyclists

John Foss: World Record holder for many unicycling events.

Kaleigh Grainger: British unicyclist

Kris Holm: Pioneer in Mountain Unicycling

Chris Carter: The "King of Unicycling" and SE unicycling revolutionist

International Championships-UNICON

International Championships (UNICON)consists of unicycle track & field- high jump, long jump, racing, (1 foot, wheelwalk, coasting, juggling etc.) slowboard and the obstacle course. Freestyle Events Include: Pairs, Individual, Club, Group, and Standard Skills (Where the rider must have straight arms and perform skills)

UNICON is held every two years. The most current UNICON was in 2006 in Langenthal, Switzerland.

10

Air Hockey

Air hockey is a game for two competing players trying to score points in the opposing player's goal. Air hockey requires an air hockey table, two mallets, and a puck. A typical air hockey table consists of a large smooth playing surface, a surrounding rail to prevent the puck and mallets from leaving the table, and slots in the rail at either end of the table that serve as goals. On the ends of the table behind and below the goals, there is usually a puck return. Additionally, tables will typically have some sort of machinery that produces a cushion of air on the play surface, with the purpose of reducing friction and increasing play speed.

In some tables, the machinery is eschewed in favour of a slick table surface, usually plastic, in the interest of saving money in both manufacturing and maintenance costs. Note that these tables are technically not air hockey tables since no air is involved, however, they are still generally understood to be as such due to the basic similarity of gameplay.

Currently, the only tables that are approved for play and sanctioned by the USAA (United States Air-Table-Hockey Association) for tournament play are 8-foot tables manufactured by Dynamo. Approved tables include the Photon, Pro-Style, older Blue Top, Brown Top, Purple

Top or Black Top with unpainted rails. The HotFlash 2 and other full-size commercial tables with neon lights and/or painted rails are not approved for USAA play but are still great tables on which to learn the games

A mallet (sometimes called a goalie, striker or paddle) consists of a simple handle attached to a flat surface that will usually lie flush with the surface of the table. The most common mallets, called "high-tops", resemble small plastic sombreros, but other mallets, "flat-tops", are used with a shorter nub.

Air Hockey pucks are slim discs made of a plastic material known as Lexan. Standard USAA-approved pucks are the yellow lexan, red lexan and the Dynamo green. In competitive play, a layer of thin white tape is placed on the face-up side.

Game play

Here are some basic rules as defined by the USAA:

— A face-off or coin toss decides which player gets the first possession of the puck.

— The first person to score 7 points by shooting the puck into the opponent's goal wins the game. When the puck breaks the horizontal plane inside the goal, a point is counted, whether or not captured by the electronic scoring device.

— Once the puck is on a certain player's side of the center line, he/she has 7 seconds to hit the puck back across the center line. Otherwise a foul is committed and the opponent receives possession of the puck.

— Placing one's mallet on top of the puck, known as topping, is a foul. Here the opponent receives possession of the puck.

— A player cannot touch or strike the puck with any part of his/her body or with any object other than the mallet. Doing so causes a foul and possession changes hands.

— If the puck is on a clear path into the goal and the player stops it with anything other than the mallet, this is goaltending. Here the opponent receives a free shot.

— Hitting the puck when it is on the opposite side of the center line, or crossing the center line completely with one's mallet causes a foul. Here the opponent receives possession of the puck.

— If the puck leaves the table, a foul is called on the player that caused the puck to go out of play due to offensive motion and the opposing player gets possession of the puck. Generally, when a player causes the puck to leave the table with a forward motion of the mallet, even defensively (known as charging), the foul is charged on them. An out of play foul results in the opponent receiving possession of the puck.

Tips from the professionals

— Grip the mallet behind the knob using your fingertips, not on top of it. This will allow more wrist action and help you be able to move the mallet around the table faster.

— For basic defence, keep your mallet centered about 8-10 inches out from the goal. From that point, very slight movements to the left and right will block virtually all straight shots. Pull back quickly to the corners of the goal to block the bank shots. This is known as the "triangle defence".

— Gain control of the puck before you take a shot. Shots are often hit out of "drifts", where the puck travels in set patterns designed to throw off your opponent's expectations and timing. The most popular drifts are the "center", "diamond", "diagonal", and "L". After establishing your drift, set up your shots like you would set up a shot in a game of pool— take your time, figure out where you want to shoot, aim and fire!

— Practice "combos": these are groups of shots which are hit with the same apparent delivery but opposite locations, caused by hitting the puck at slightly different locations on the mallet. For example, a transverse motion of the right arm can lead to a "cut shot" to the left corner of the opponent's goal or a "right wall under" (bank off the right wall, into the right corner of the opponent's goal). Keep your opponent guessing!

— There are many ways to get around your opponent's defence. Aim for the corners of the goal. On bank shots, try to get the puck in the goal off of a one-wall bank. If you hit double or triple banks, the puck loses velocity and will be easy to block.

History

Air hockey was invented by Bob Lemieux, an avid ice hockey fan and engineer at Brunswick Billiards in 1972. It was an immediate financial success, and by the mid-1970's there arose substantial interest in tournament play. To ensure uniform play standards of the highest competitive quality, the United States Air-Table Hockey Association (USAA) was formed in 1978 by J. Phillip "Phil" Arnold, largely as an official sanctioning body. Since its inception, the USAA has sanctioned at least one national-level or World championship each year, crowning 12 different champions over 30 years.

The USAA remains at present the only recognized worldwide player organisation for air hockey, and has maintained a close relationship with table manufacturers and event promoters over the years. Today, competitive air hockey is played by a close-knit community of serious players around the world, with extensive player bases near Houston, San Francisco, Los Angeles, Denver, Chicago, New York, Maryland and Boston in the United States, Barcelona and Seville in Spain, Saint Petersburg and Moscow in Russia and Most in the Czech Republic. From the late 1980's, Caracas, Venezuela served as a hotbed of activity; three-time World Champion Jose Mora, and other finalists originated from there. By 1999 most of the Venezuelan activity had disappeared; however, re-emergence is expected with the return of former champion Pedro Otero from Spain.

11

Under Water Hockey

Underwater hockey (also called Octopush) is a non-contact sport in which two teams compete to maneuver a puck across the bottom of a swimming pool into goals.

Underwater Hockey Equipment

Players wear a diving mask, fins, and a snorkel for play. Safety gear includes a water polo style cap, a mouthguard, and a glove for the playing hand (to protect against pool-bottom abrasion and, in some designs, knuckle protection against puck impact). Because current rules permit a player to switch the stick between hands mid-play, players may choose to wear a protective glove on both hands. The stick is quite short (according to recent rules, not more than 350mm. in length, including the handle) and is coloured white or black to indicate the player's team. In tournament play, the colour of the stick, swimwear and cap are randomly assigned to each teams before every game.

The puck is approximately the size of an ice hockey puck but is made of lead or similar material and is surrounded by a plastic covering, which is usually matched to the pool bottom to facilitate good grip on the stick face while preventing excessive friction on the pool bottom. The puck's weight brings it to rest on the pool bottom, though can be lofted during passes. The goals are three meters in width and lie at opposite ends of the playing area.

Play

Two teams of up to ten players compete, with six players on each team in play at once. Substitution happens continually from a substitution area, which may be on deck or in the water outside the playing area, depending on tournament rules. Before the start of play the puck is placed in the middle of the pool, and the players wait in the water, touching the wall above the goals they are defending. At the start-of-play signal, in-play members of both teams are free to swim anywhere in the play area and try to score by sending the puck into the opponents' goal. Play continues until either a goal is scored, and players return to their wall to start a new point, or a break in play is signalled by a referee (whether due to a foul, a time-out, or the end of the period of play).

The most typical playing formation in the US is the 3-3 (three offensive players or forwards, and three defensive players or backs). Other options include 2-3-1 (i.e., two forwards, three midfielders, and a back), 1-3-2, or 2-2-2. As important to tournament teams' formation strategy is the substitution strategy: which players will substitute for which positions, and how many players are substituting for how many positions. A 10-member team playing 3-3, for example, may have two players substituting for each other at the center-forward position, three players covering the other two forward positions, and five players covering the three defensive positions. Substitution errors might result in a foul (too many players in the play area) or a tactical blunder (too few defenders in on a play).

There are a number of penalties described in the official underwater hockey rules, ranging from use of the stick against something (or someone) other than the puck or the playing surface, playing or stopping the puck with something other than the stick, and "screening" (interposing one's self between a teammate who possesses the puck and an opponent; one is allowed to play the puck, but not merely block opponents with one's body).

If the penalty is minor, referees award an advantage puck -- the team that committed the foul is pushed back 3 meters from the puck, while the other team gets a free possession. For major penalties, such as a dangerous pass (.e.g., over an opponent's shoulder near the head) or intentional or repeated fouls, the referees may eject players for a specified period of time or the remainder of the game. A defender committing a serious foul sufficiently close to his own goal may be penalised by the award of a point to the fouled player's team.

Games consist of two halves, typically ten to fifteen minutes in length (depending on tournament rules; 15 minutes at world championship tournaments) and a short half time interval. At half time the two teams switch ends.

Referees

Refereeing the game are two (or three) "water refs" (referees in the pool with full snorkelling gear, and usually a distinctive refs cap and t-shirt) to observe and referee play at the pool bottom, and one or more poolside "deck refs" to track time (both in the period and for each ejected player), maintain the score, and call fouls (such as excessive number of players in play, failure to start a point from the end of the playing area, or another foul capable of being committed at or noticed at the surface).

The "deck ref" responds to hand signals given by the water refs to start and stop play, including after an interruption such as a foul or time-out.

Spectators

Underwater Hockey is not spectator friendly. Since the action is all below the surface, one must enter the water to get the full effect of the game. Spectators may either try on fins, a snorkel, and mask and enter the pool for a view of the playing area, or take advantage of the work of underwater videographers who have recorded major tournaments. Organisers of major tournaments are usually the only contacts for acquiring underwater hockey footage, and no official worldwide repository exists for recorded games. However, there is a growing collection of underwater videos at video repositories such as YouTube and Google Video.

Filming the games is challenging even for the experienced videographer, as the players' movement is fast and there is no place on the surface or beneath it which is free from the frenzied movement of the players, however research & development of filming techniques is ongoing, through such projects as See The Game.

High level World Championship Events, in most of the past years has attempted video of the games. The latest attempt during the 2006 Championship in Sheffield, England even included online streamed footage via a commercial company UK Worlds Web-Site.

History

The sport was invented in 1954 and first played by four divers from Southsea, England: John Ventham, Alan Blake, Jack Willis, and Frank Lilleker. Originally called Octopush (and is still known primarily by that name in the United Kingdom today), the original rules called for teams of eight players (hence, "octo-"), a bat reminiscent of a tiny shuffleboard stick, called a "pusher" (hence, the "-push"), an uncoated lead puck called a "squid", and a goal known at first as a "cuttle" but soon thereafter a "gully".

The first rules were tested in a 1954 two-on-two game, and an announcement was made in the November, 1954 issue of Neptune. The object of the game was to keep members of British Sub-Aqua Club #9 from abandoning the new club during the winter months in which it was too cold to dive the North Sea. The substantial changes in equipment, team size, and other factors have helped make the game the international sport it is today.

The game first came to Canada (and probably to North America) in 1962 via Norm Liebeck, a decidedly unconventional Australian scuba diving instructor and dive shop owner, who introduced the sport to the Vanquatics, a Vancouver dive club previously named the Wobbygongs. Ten years later, the Underwater Hockey Association of British Columbia (UHABC) was formed and received support from the BC government.

Underwater hockey enjoys popularity in Canada, Great Britain, Australia, New Zealand, South Africa, the Netherlands and France, and can be found in numerous additional countries catalogued at The Underwater Hockey Tourist, which has catered to the needs of traveling underwater hockey players since 1996.

The world championships are held every two years in an event sanctioned by the World Underwater Federation (Conféderation Mondiale des Activités Subaquatiques, or "CMAS"). At the 2006 World Underwater Hockey Championships held in August in Sheffield, England, 48 teams competed in six age and gender categories, including teams from Australia,

Canada, Colombia, France, Italy, Japan, the Netherlands, Belgium, South Africa, Spain, Turkey, the United Kingdom of Great Britain and Northern Ireland, the Republic of Ireland, and the United States of America. Winners of the elite divisions [therefore current world champions] were Australia in women's division, and New Zealand in men's division. New Zealand is the strongest underwater hockey nation in the world, winning three of the six divisions.

12

A History of the Rule of Hockey

Research into the history of the Rules of Hockey was undertaken to mark the centenary of the formation of the Hockey Rules Board and to recognise the leading part played by the Board in ensuring that hockey players at all levels have been able to enjoy their game under controlled, authoritative, yet user-friendly, world-wide Rules.

The general changes to Rules and therefore is not a complete list of all changes. It is based on the Rules of hockey produced for men's hockey and therefore does not include details of the Rules for women's hockey before the Rules were combined into one common code in 1975.

A set of Rules was actually drawn up by several clubs in London in January 1876 following the establishment of the first, but short lived, Hockey Association (of England) the year before. (The second, and final, Hockey Association was formed in 1886.) Prior to that date the captains had agreed the Rules under which each game was played, including the number of players per team which varied from eight to eleven.

Chronology

The "Surbiton" rules included the following:

- the pitch was between 100 and 150 yards long and between 50 and 80 yards wide; goals consisted of 7 feet tall posts placed 6 yards part with a "tape" stretched across the top of the posts;
- the sticks were "curved wooden ones approved by the Committee of the Association" and the ball was an "ordinary sized cricket ball";
- offside is specified as requiring three opponents to be nearer their own goal-line and applies throughout the pitch except when the ball is hit from the goal-line;
- if the ball goes out of play over the side-line (described in these rules as being "in touch") play was restarted by rolling the ball back into the field at right angles to the line;
- players were not permitted to raise their stick above their shoulder;
- a circle does not seem to be marked on the pitch but the rules do say that "no goals shall be allowed if the ball be hit from a distance of more than 15 yards from the nearest goalpost";
- if a rule was infringed "the ball shall be brought back and a bully shall take place";
- some typical hockey actions were referred to in these rules but not defined; for example, a bully starts the game but there is no specification of how a bully is conducted;
- another example is that the flat playing side of the stick is not defined but the rules do say that "the ball shall be played from right to left".

The Hockey Association (England) drew up a code of Rules based on those used by clubs in the London area including Surbiton as noted above. These included:

— the pitch should be 100 yards long by 55 to 60 yards wide; goals should be 4 yards wide with a cross bar 7 feet from the ground; there would be a striking circle with a radius of 15 yards; flags (not lines) indicated the 25 yards area;

— the game was to be started (and re-started after a goal) by a bully which involved three taps of the stick between two players at the centre spot; a bully would also be taken at 25 yards after the ball had gone over the back-line;

— all non-involved players had to be 5 yards from the ball at free hits, rolls-in and bullies; rolls-in by hand were used to put the ball into play after it had gone over the side-line;

— teams comprised eleven players - five forwards, three half-backs, two full-backs and one goalkeeper; no substitutes were allowed even for injury;

— the game was controlled either by two umpires or one umpire (referee) assisted by two linesmen;

— hockey sticks were made of wood with leather-covered handles;

— balls used were traditional leather-covered cricket balls painted white;

— there was no mention of goalkeepers equipment;

— the ball was played with one side of the stick (the left hand side) only; the ball could not be played above the shoulder or with the rounded side (back) of the stick;

— it was not permitted to kick, trip, shove, or obstruct an opponent;

— hands and feet could be used to stop the ball but then had to be moved out of the way; feet and legs could not to be used behind the ball to resist opponents;

— goalkeepers could kick the ball but only within their own circles;

— hooking of sticks was allowed but only within striking distance of the ball;

— offside (with less than 3 defenders) was applied from the half-way line;

— a bully was taken in the circle for an offence by a defender; free hits were given for other fouls.

1886: The Hockey Association decreed that a stick must pass through a two inch measurement ring; sticks could have a four inch external diameter India rubber ring above the splice to prevent finger injuries.

1894: Reverse stick play was permitted as were shots at goal without first stopping the ball.

1900: The International Rules Board (later the Hockey Rules Board) was formed on 23 April 1900 in London by the men's Hockey Associations of England, Ireland and Wales; the Rules of the Game were decided thereafter by the Board. The first meeting of the International Rules Board was held on the 25 July 1900.

1900: Advantage was recognised; not every offence was to be penalised immediately.

1900: Scotland's Men's Association joined the Board.

1904: Intentional undercutting and raising the ball from a hit was to be penalised. The scoop stroke was permitted.

1905: Each umpire was to take half of the pitch for the whole game without changing ends and to take decisions on rolls-in for the whole of their side-line, but not for corners. Umpires were also empowered to warn and/or suspend players from the game. A weight limit of 28 ounces was laid down for sticks. The width of the pitch could be up to 66 yards.

1907: Umpires were allowed to apply the Rules without waiting for an appeal. Prior to this time appeals had to be made by players before an umpire could give a decision.

1908: The penalty corner was introduced for offences by defenders in the circle. At a penalty corner, the Rules required the ball to be stopped before a shot at goal but this was not umpired rigorously. All defenders were behind the goal-line with attacking players outside the circle. The bully was replaced by a penalty bully for deliberately stopping a certain goal.

1909: The width of the pitch reverted to 55 to 60 yards.

1910: Goalposts were specified as 2 inches deep and not more than 3 inches wide.

1927: Advantage was formally written as Rule. By this time there were routinely two umpires for each match.

1936:Notes and suggestions for umpires were included in the Rules book. Later this became an appendix entitled 'Advice to Umpires'.

1938: Any form of interference with the stick of an opponent, including hooking of sticks, was forbidden as was the use of any part of the body, except the hand, to stop the ball.

1949: Deliberate offences by defenders within the 25 yards area and persistent offences by defenders at corners were penalised by a penalty corner.

1949: The radius of the circle was increased to 16 yards (but this was not incorporated in the women's game until 1968).

1957: The 25 yards bully after a ball had gone over the back line was replaced by a free hit at 16 yards.

1959: Umpires were empowered to suspend players for a temporary period.

1961: At a penalty corner and for corners, a maximum of six defenders were to be behind the back line with the remainder of the defending team at the 25 yards line.

1963: The penalty bully was replaced by a penalty stroke taken from a spot 8 yards from the goal. For a penalty corner, the remainder of the defending team were moved to be behind the centre (and not just the 25 yards) line.

1970: The roll-in from side-line was replaced by a push-in.

1972: Offside was changed from three to two defenders.

1973: Two substitutes were permitted but once substituted a player was not permitted to return.

1974: A penalty stroke was to be awarded for a deliberate offence by a defender in the circle, regardless of whether a goal might have been scored or not.

1975: The first common Rule book for men and women was published. Changes made at this time included:

— at a penalty corner the ball was to be stopped motionless by an attacker before a shot at goal; there was to be no latitude;

— notes on the Rules became 'Guidance for Players and Umpires';

— a code of signals for umpires was published for the first time;

— a temporary suspension for offending player(s) was to be at least 5 minutes;

— the width of the pitch was specified as 60 yards;

— a note to the Rules had previously stated that matches did not necessarily have to be played on grass provided that the surface was suitable; in recognition of the growing use of synthetic surfaces, this was deleted with no mention of particular playing surfaces in the Rules;

— the penalty stroke spot was moved from 8 to 7 yards from the goal-line.

1979: Colour control cards (green, yellow, red) were introduced into the Rules book (although they had been in general use for a number of years). Flags were removed from the 25 yards line.

1983: Various changes included:

— a hit-in replaced the push-in from the side line;

— a pass back replaced the centre bully to start or restart the game;

— the bully was retained only for accidents or unforeseen events;

— the Rule explicitly limiting the height to which the stick could be raised was deleted; this would in future be dealt with under dangerous play;

— the use of the hand except by a goalkeeper was abolished;

— at free hits only opponents had to be 5 yards from the ball

— no free hits to the attacking team were to be taken within five yards of the circle.

1984: The "long" corner was changed from being similar to the penalty corner to instead essentially being a free hit taken from a spot on the goal-line within 5 yards of the corner flag with all players (other than the striker) at least 5 yards from the ball.

1986: Definitions of 'Hockey Terminology' were included for the first time.

1987: Again, a number of changes:

— the number of defenders behind the back line at penalty corners was reduced from six to five;
— at corners and 16 yard hits only opponents were required to be 5 yards from the ball;
— at penalty corners the first hit at goal should not cross the goal-line higher than 18 inches and if the ball travelled more than 5 yards outside the circle then the penalty corner Rules no longer applied;
— the penalty corner was finished after the ball the ball travelled 5 yards from the outer edge of the circle;
— offside applied only in the 25 yards area;
— a deliberately raised ball falling into the circle was to be penalised;
— free hits to defenders could be taken within the circle;
— at free hits to the attacking team within five yards of the circle all players had to be five yards from the ball.

1988: 'Technical Interpretations' were published as an appendix to the Rules book.

1989: The maximum number of permitted substitutes was increased from two to three. Goalkeepers were permitted to stop the ball with the stick above the shoulder in their circle.

1992: Substitution ('rolling substitutes') could take place at any time during the game. A team now officially consisted of sixteen players but with only eleven (including a goalkeeper) allowed on the field of play at any one time. Interpretation of obstruction was revised.

1994: Captains were made responsible for their team's behaviour and for substitutions. Goalkeepers were required to wear protective headgear.

1995: The format of the Rule book was revised to make it more user friendly. Also:

— at a free hit the ball was required to move at least 1 yard;

— umpires were empowered to order a free hit to be advanced by 10 yards for dissent or a subsequent offence;

— goalkeepers were permitted to deflect (in addition to stop as hitherto) a ball above their shoulder;

— substitution was allowed at penalty corners and penalty strokes;

— the ball was put back into play at a penalty corner from a spot exactly 10 yards from the goal-post and not at least 10 yards as hitherto.

1996: Changes included:

— at a penalty corner the ball had to be stopped outside the circle before a shot at goal could be made;

— the pass-back to start or restart the game became a centre pass which could be played in any direction;

— goalkeepers' gauntlets were re-named 'hand protectors' with a maximum length of 9 inches and a maximum width of 14 inches.

Mandatory Experimental Rules introduced were:

— no offside;

— players may not intentionally enter their opponents goal, stand on their opponents goal-line or intentionally run behind either goal;

— a corner to be taken on a spot on the side line 5 yards from the corner flag;

— within the 25 yards area all players, except the taker, to be 5 yards from the ball at free hits, hits-in and 16 yards hits.

1997: A mandatory experimental Rule required the prolongation of play to permit the completion of a penalty corner at half-time and full-time.

1998: The 1996 mandatory experimental Rules concerning no offside, players not intentionally entering their opponents goal and a corner taken on the side line were confirmed as Rules. The experiment concerning free hits within the 25 yards area was abandoned. Other changes included:

— substitutions at penalty corners were no longer permitted except for an injured defending goalkeeper but were still permitted at penalty strokes;

— all measurements and distances were now stated in metric form with an imperial-metric conversion table included at the end of the Rules book;

— 'Technical Information and Advice' was published as an appendix

— metric rather than imperial measurements and distances.

1999: Changes included:

— acknowledgement of a continuing study of the composition of the stick but metal and metallic substances were already banned;

— a mandatory experimental Rule allowing use of the edge (but not the rounded side) of the stick subject to the normal safety considerations;

— clarification of the Rule when a goalkeeper is suspended at a penalty corner; another goalkeeper must be the replacement with the team consequently having to withdraw one field player until the period of suspension is completed;

— the 1997 mandatory experimental Rule to require prolongation of time for completion of a penalty corner at half-time and full-time was confirmed as a Rule.

2000: **Changes were:**

— more precise specification of the shape, size, weight and material of the stick; it may be made of wood or may contain any other material except metal or metallic components;

— a broken white line to be marked on the pitch 5 metres from and beyond the circle line;

— the ball was put back into play at a penalty corner from a spot on the back-line inside the circle and at least 9.14 metres (10 yards) from the goal-post.

2001: The mandatory experiment allowing the edge of the stick to be used to play the ball entered its third year but it was announced that it would be incorporated as a formal Rules change with effect from 2002.

Changes were relatively minor and included:

— moving the short distance markings from inside to outside the field of play to avoid undue and uneven wear especially on synthetic pitch surfaces;

— a re-wording of the specification of the stick to make it clearer;

— allowing that a captain can be on the field of play or, at particular times in the game, can be a substitute;

— a new Rule which specifically makes a manufactured foul an offence;

— limiting goalkeepers to playing in their own defending half of the pitch.'

2002: Changes to the Rules were few this year: using the edge of the stick to play the ball was confirmed as a formal Rule and when the penalty corner is completed for substitution purposes was clarified.

The Rules interpretations in the appendix to the Rules were revised. Before this date various formal and informal papers advising umpires on the required interpretations had been published especially at major competitions. The aim was to incorporate these in the Rules Book so that interpretations were more consistent throughout the game.

2003: For the first time in many years a full Rules Book was not published. This was because the FIH had decided to move to a standard date of 1 January annually for implementation of Rules change whereas each set of Rules had in the past taken effect from various dates mid-year. However, two Mandatory Experimental Rules were implemented from 1 January 2003 so a small leaflet was produced to provide details:

— defenders were permitted to use their stick above their shoulder to stop or deflect a shot at goal;

— it was no longer necessary to stop the ball outside the circle before a shot could be taken at a penalty corner but, instead, the ball was only required to travel outside the circle.

This *History of the Rules of Hockey* is based on a *Chronology of the Rules of Hockey* researched and produced on behalf of the Hockey Rules Board by Ernest Wall, Evlyn Raistrick and George Croft in 2000 to mark the centenary of the establishment of the International Rules Board which subsequently became the Hockey Rules Board.

2004: This year saw the publication of a radically revised Rules Book. The Rules had been completely re-written to make them easier to understand. The layout changed so that the Rules were in just two sections:

— Playing the Game
— Umpiring.

Detailed technical specifications of the field, stick, ball and equipment were omitted from the main publication and published separately.

The opportunity was taken to simplify a few Rules without changing any of the fundamental characteristics of the game. The adjustments included:

— simplifying and standardising how a penalty corner is completed for substitution purposes and at the end of half-time and full-time;
— requiring field players who leave the field for injury treatment, refreshment, to change equipment or for some reason other than substitution to re-enter only between the 23 metres areas;
— specifying how the result of a match is decided;
— rationalising procedures for starting and re-starting play so that the procedures for taking a free hit also apply to the centre pass and to putting the ball back into play after it has passed completely over the side-line or back-line;
— retaining the fundamental characteristics of the bully but simplifying it by requiring sticks to touch only once;
— deleting the Rule which specified that a ball must not be raised intentionally so that it lands directly in the circle was deleted;
— simplifying the obstruction Rule by referring in the Rule itself only to the fundamental principle that players must not obstruct an opponent who is attempting to play the ball;
— specifying that players must not tackle unless they are in a position to play the ball without body contact;

— specifying the 'advantage Rule' more simply and clearly;

— requiring the player taking a penalty stroke to start by standing behind and within playing distance of the ball and not permitting them to approach either the ball or the goalkeeper after taking the stroke (ie the former limitation of taking only one step forward was deleted);

— specifying that the whistle must be blown to start a penalty stroke when both players are in position (rather than requiring the umpire to confirm that both are ready which can cause confusion in the absence of a common spoken language);

— rationalising how offences at a penalty stroke are dealt with; it was specified that the penalty stroke is taken again if a goalkeeper prevents a goal being scored but leaves the goal-line or moves either foot before the ball was played;

— permitting the intended duration of a temporary suspension to be extended for misconduct by a player while suspended;

— introducing new umpiring signals to indicate dangerous play (placing one forearm diagonally across the chest) and stick obstruction (holding one arm out and downwards in front of the body half-way between vertical and horizontal; touching the forearm with the other hand).

In addition, the two Mandatory Experimental Rules introduced in 2003 continued to apply in 2004. They were:

— permitting a defender to use the stick to stop or deflect a shot at goal at any height.

— not requiring the ball to be stopped before a shot at goal at a penalty corner.

2005: The main change this year was that the two Mandatory Experimental Rules referred to above were incorporated as formal rules of the game.

In addition, the field, stick, ball and equipment specifications were re-incorporated in the main rules publication instead of being published separately as in 2004. Otherwise, there were only minor clarifications of the wording of some rules.

2006: The only change this year was to the maximum bow/rake permitted in the stick. It was reduced from 50mm to 25mm. The reason quoted was a concern about an increase in the power with which some players could flick the ball, especially for shots at goal, using an extremely bowed stick.

2007/8: a significant change was the move to a two-year cycle for the production and publication of the rules of the game. In some ways, a two-year cycle was already in place because significant changes were not introduced in the periods leading to each Olympic Games and Hockey World Cup. By formalising this cycle, the Hockey Rules Board (HRB) was also acknowledging that it is better to allow a slightly longer period between rules changes for any such changes to be evaluated and reviewed.

Specific changes included:

— permitting a team either to have a goalkeeper on the field (with full protective equipment or only with protective headgear) or to play entirely with field players (in which case no player has goalkeeping privileges).

— specifying the face protection which field players are permitted to wear especially in relation to defending a penalty corner.

— prohibiting hitting the ball hard on the forehand with the edge of the stick.

— clarifying that a defender must not be penalised if their stick is not motionless or is travelling towards the ball while attempting to stop or deflect the shot even when the ball is above shoulder height.

— permitting a goalkeeper to use their hands, arms or any other part of their body (and not just their stick, kickers and leg-guards as hitherto) to move the ball away but only as part of a goal saving action and not to propel the ball forcefully so that it travels a long distance.

Early Indoor Rules

Until 1966, the German Hockey Associations, in both West Germany and East Germany, had been producing a rules book for their domestic use which was used, after translation, by other European countries but not, at that time, by Great Britain.

The then Honorary General Secretary of the FIH, Rene Frank, later FIH President, was a keen supporter of the game not only in his native Belgium but also elsewhere in Europe. He regularly attended the Cities Tournament sponsored by the West Berlin Senate and after the formation of the FIH Indoor Hockey Committee attended their meetings which were also usually held in Berlin.

FIH Indoor Hockey Committee

In 1966, Rene Frank persuaded the Germans to hand over responsibility for the rules to the FIH Indoor Hockey Committee, which at that time had several German officials as members. Accordingly in 1966 the FIH Office in Brussels produced the first FIH Indoor Rules Book in three languages, German, French and English. Significantly, in 1968 the FIH recognised the indoor game by decreeing in its Constitution that hockey included indoor hockey.

The FIH Indoor Hockey Committee continued to be responsible for the Indoor Rules Book and its printing via the Brussels office, until responsibility for the indoor rules was transferred in 1988 to the Hockey Rules Board. The FIH Indoor Hockey Committee was also abolished in 1988 and the European Hockey Federation took over its responsibilities for competitions in Europe.

Rules of Indoor Hockey

Before setting out the rules' changes since 1966, it is only proper to reproduce here Rene Frank's Preface to the three-language edition. 'The International Hockey Federation takes pleasure in presenting this booklet with the official Rules of Indoor Hockey in three languages: English, French and German. In order to make these rules easier to study and to apply, their wording has been entirely modified by the FIH Indoor Hockey Committee. Many notes and explanations are also included in the new text.

The Game of Indoor Hockey which is 15 years old only, has spread quickly and its number of players is ever increasing. We want to stress the usefulness of this very fast and attractive game for Field Hockey players. As a matter of fact it gives them the opportunity to improve by playing more frequently and allows also those belonging to countries where it is difficult or impossible to play Field Hockey in the Winter to practise their favourite sport.

We hope that this first edition of the official Indoor Hockey Rules shall be welcomed, also that it will serve the Game and contribute to the improvement of umpiring' Basically the rules taken over by the FIH are still those in force today and included the provision that all rules of outdoor (field) hockey not mentioned or altered by the indoor rules shall also apply to indoor hockey.

First Indoor Rules

— Six players, including a goalkeeper and a maximum of six substitutes, but only at specific situations in the game.

— If any team was reduced to less than four players, the opponents were declared the winners.

— Dimensions of pitch and goals (slightly smaller than those of outdoor hockey) ~ indoor rules have always been in metric terms.

— Hits not allowed – pushes only and no raised ball except when shooting at goal; goalkeepers not permitted to raise the ball when kicking it.

— At penalty corners only the defending goalkeeper was permitted to stand in the goal until the ball was pushed out, with the other five players being required to stand outside the goal behind the back line on the opposite side from where the ball was being played - they could, after the ball was played, move into the goal-mouth.

— The game was to be played on any hard, fast surface. Players' footwear and equipment were specified and goalkeepers' gloves were to be the same as for outdoor hockey.

— No offside and no corners.

— Playing time (originally 2 x 15 minutes) was increased to 2 x 20 minutes with lesser time for junior domestic matches.

Several rules, of course, followed the basic principles of outdoor hockey including the stick and the ball although later the indoor ball was required to be seamless.

However in 1986 when it appeared that the indoor game seemed to be departing in some respects from hockey in general the rules book was re-written to conform as closely as possible, where appropriate, to the rules and their wording of outdoor hockey.

Interestingly enough, one indoor rule in 1966 provided for a penalty stroke from 7 metres to be awarded for 'any grave and unsporting behaviour by a team in its own half of the ground'. Also, there was the rule providing that a penalty corner be awarded for a deliberate offence within a player's own half, and that still remains. In 1966 however, a player could be temporarily suspended 'for unsporting behaviour' for two to five minutes or be suspended for the remainder of the game and an incapacitated or suspended goalkeeper had to be replaced by another goalkeeper.

Finally, the use of the hand to stop the ball in the air during play or at penalty corners by players other than the goalkeeper was permitted until 1992.

Accordingly, what occurred in rule changes after 1966 fell into two categories. One for reasons of clearer interpretation and requirements of the game as it became more international and thus more sophisticated and the other to keep in line with outdoor hockey rules but only where appropriate. The first FIH authorised tournament matches occurred in 1972, with a European Nations Cup for men in 1973 and a women's championship in 1975.

1974:

— Players must not stand in their opponents' goal mouth.

— Time prolonged at half-time and full-time to allow penalty corners to be completed, supported by a definition as to when such an award was ended.

— Prior to a revised edition in 1976 - the provision to

forbid substitutions after the award of a penalty corner or penalty stroke.

1975/6:

— A player's stick must be on the ground when playing the ball for a shot at goal.

— A player may not hit or play the ball in the air (but could stop it).

— Players may not take part in the game whilst lying on the pitch except for goalkeepers within their own circles, introduced because players were lying on the pitch thus reducing the playing area and causing unwanted obstruction.

1978:

— An injured player was permitted to be substituted during normal play (but only the injured player).

— It was also made clear that an umpire's jurisdiction also extended to all players including those occupying the team benches.

1979:

— The substitution of a goalkeeper by a field player with the privileges of a goalkeeper but who was required to wear a different coloured shirt from that of all other players – recognising what had been happening for some time.

— A provision was inserted to permit substitution of incapacitated goalkeepers at penalty corners and penalty strokes.

— The coloured card procedure (green, yellow, red) was formally introduced into the Indoor Rules Book and if a bench player received a yellow card, their team had to withdraw a player until the suspension time was

— Permitting a shot at goal after the ball had been stopped (by hand or stick) either inside or outside the circle.

— At a free push all opposition players to be at least three metres from the ball thus giving the taker the opportunity to play to a colleague alongside them.

— For all free pushes within three metres of the circle, all players had to be three metres from the ball.

— Free pushes for the ball going over the side-boards could be taken up to one metre from the boards.

In 1984, Notes of Guidance for Umpires and a Code of Signals were added.

1986:

A total revision of the rules book appeared based on that of the outdoor rules book and included Guidance and Advice for Players and Umpires; Hockey Terminology; specifications on pitch marking, general and personal equipment; and many more notes and guidance on many of the rules.

— No player (except the goalkeeper) to play with knees, arms or hands on the pitch in the act of playing the ball or stopping it at penalty corners.

— In normal play the hand holding the stick was permitted to be on the pitch for tackling purposes.

— Goalkeepers were not permitted to play the ball outside the circle whilst lying on the ground.

— Players were now not permitted to deliberately enter within (as well as stand in) an opponents' goal mouth, or run behind the goals.

Hockey Rules Board First Edition

1988: The first edition, under the authority of the Hockey Rules Board included further clarification of the legitimate stop at penalty corners and made minor amendments and clarifications, many again in line with developments in outdoor hockey.

1990-92: Interpretations included in the Indoor Rule Book.

— The award of a penalty stroke for unsporting behaviour in a player's half of the pitch was deleted as it was agreed that umpires now had sufficient authority and rules' provision to deal with this.

— Requirements relating to personal equipment, including helmets used by goalkeepers.

— Goalkeepers allowed to stop the ball with their stick above their shoulder.

— Field players, when acting as goalkeepers, not permitted to wear helmets outside the circle but compulsory for defending penalty corners and penalty strokes, 1992.

The Hockey Rules Board brought indoor hockey in line with the outdoor game by abolishing all use of the hand except by goalkeepers defending their goal including also abolishing the hand stop at penalty corners. This was somewhat controversial as it was pointed out by indoor hockey followers that this would prevent a legitimate high shot at goal being stopped by hand by a field player at penalty corners. However, the rule has now found general acceptance given the fact that hockey was to be regarded as a stick and ball game.

In 1992, the push stroke was closely defined in order to stamp out the unwanted features of the dragged push stroke and dangerous follow through action.

1996: The format adopted was that which had been successful for the 1996 Outdoor Rule Book. Although the layout was extensively revised only minor changes were made to the actual indoor rules themselves, many of them just to confirm changes which had become necessary in the outdoor game. In this connection the most important alteration was to introduce the rule concerning blood injuries and blood on clothing which provided that players must leave the pitch for treatment and if necessary, change of clothing.

Other rule changes in 1996 were as follows.

— Centre pass to start or re-start the game in any direction.

— The free push must move at least 10 centimetres before another player of the same team can play the ball and it did not need not be taken on the exact spot of the offence but within playing distance.

— Goalkeepers permitted to wear 'hand protectors' which were no longer referred to as gauntlets or with any reference to fingers and which were subject to size limitations (23 centimetres wide and 35.5 centimetres long).

— The obstruction rule was simplified and included holding the ball against the side-board as an offence.

The new 1996 book also included Technical Advice, an innovation introduced to assist National Associations in their endeavours to start up or improve indoor hockey facilities. Advice was provided on such matters as flooring, lighting, pitch size and pitch furniture.

One notable change to the outdoor rules not transferred to the indoor game was the continuous substitutions' provisions including permission to substitute at penalty corners and penalty strokes. It was decided that such a change would be detrimental to the control of indoor play and accordingly the existing substitution controls were confirmed.

After the 1996 edition, some very minor alterations to the indoor rules were made for clarification, but it was not deemed necessary to reprint the rules book itself. In 1998, the FIH decree, recommended by the Hockey Rules Board and the FIH Equipment Committee, that hockey sticks must no longer contain any metallic substances, was incorporated into indoor hockey. It was also decided to incorporate into the indoor rules the experimental but mandatory provision to permit the ball to be played by the edge of the stick in appropriate indoor situations.

2000: At its February 2000 meeting, the Hockey Rules Board, apart from updating some of the text to conform to the current rules of outdoor hockey, agreed the various new rules and alterations to existing provisions, again bringing the indoor and outdoor rules closer together.

— Stick specification was agreed - a diagram of the stick was included in the Indoor Rule Book.
— A mandatory experiment relating to play with the edge of the stick.
— Substitution of an attacker or defender permitted at the award of a Penalty Stroke.
— The captain's responsibility for team discipline was increased to include substitutes.
— For a further offence before the awarded penalty has been taken, the penalty may be progressed up to five metres, upgraded and/or dealt with as misconduct, or reversed if committed by the previously benefiting team

2004: The indoor Rules adopted the radically revised approach used this year for the outdoor/field hockey Rules and therefore consisted of just two sections:

— Playing the Game
— Umpiring.

Detailed technical specifications of the pitch, stick, ball and equipment were omitted from the main publication and published separately.

This was the first update of the indoor Rules since 2000. It was therefore appropriate to incorporate the relevant minor changes which had been introduced to the outdoor Rules in the interim. The overall presentation of indoor hockey was also simplified by adopting common indoor and outdoor Rules where appropriate but retaining the distinctive characteristics of each version of the game. More generally, some minor amendments to the indoor Rules which simplify the game were incorporated.

The changes were relatively minor and in many instances were the same as those for outdoor hockey. However, for completeness in this history of the indoor Rules all the main changes are indicated below:

— in common with outdoor hockey, permitting a captain to be on the pitch or, at particular times in the match, to be a substitute;

— making the Rules governing substitution the same for indoor and outdoor hockey (ie at any time except within the period from the award of a penalty corner until after it has been completed);

— simplifying and standardising how a penalty corner is completed for substitution purposes and at the end of half-time and full-time;

— requiring field players who leave the pitch for injury treatment, refreshment, to change equipment or for some reason other than substitution to re-enter only within 3 metres of the centre-line;

— specifying how the result of a match is decided;

— rationalising procedures for starting and re-starting play so that the procedures for taking a free push also apply to the centre pass and to putting the ball back into play after it has passed completely over the side-board or back-line;

— retaining the fundamental characteristics of the bully but simplifying it by requiring sticks to touch only once;

— specifying that players must not force an opponent into offending unintentionally;

— simplifying the obstruction Rule by referring in the Rule itself only to the fundamental principle that players must not obstruct an opponent who is attempting to play the ball;

— specifying that players must not tackle unless they are in a position to play the ball without body contact;

— specifying the 'advantage Rule' more simply and clearly;

— introducing the Mandatory Experimental Rule to indoor hockey which permitted a defender to use the stick to stop or deflect a shot at goal at any height;

— introducing the Mandatory Experimental Rule to indoor hockey which specified that the ball must travel outside the circle but need not be stopped before a shot at a goal at a penalty corner; this replaced the previous requirement that the ball must be stopped or come to rest inside or outside the circle before a shot could be taken;

— requiring the player taking a penalty stroke to start by standing behind and within playing distance of the ball and not permitting them to approach either the ball or the goalkeeper after taking the stroke (ie the former limitation of taking only one step forward was deleted);

— specifying that the whistle must be blown to start a penalty stroke when both players are in position (rather than requiring the umpire to confirm that both are ready which can cause confusion in the absence of a common spoken language);

— rationalising how offences at a penalty stroke are dealt with; it was specified that the penalty stroke is taken again if a goalkeeper prevents a goal being scored but leaves the goal-line or moves either foot before the ball was played;

— permitting the intended duration of a temporary suspension to be extended for misconduct by a player while suspended;

— introducing new umpiring signals to indicate dangerous play (placing one forearm diagonally across the chest) and stick obstruction (holding one arm out and downwards in front of the body half-way between vertical and horizontal; touching the forearm with the other hand).

2005: The main change was that the two Mandatory Experimental Rules referred to above were incorporated as formal rules of the game:

— permitting a defender to use the stick to stop or deflect a shot at goal at any height;

— requiring the ball to travel outside the circle before a shot at goal at a penalty corner but not requiring it to be stopped.

In addition, the field, stick, ball and equipment specifications were re-incorporated in the main rules publication instead of being published separately as in 2004. Otherwise, there were only minor clarifications of the wording of some rules.

2006: The only change this year was to the maximum bow/rake permitted in the stick. It was reduced from 50mm to 25mm. The reason quoted was a concern about an increase in the power with which some players could flick the ball, especially for shots at goal, using an extremely bowed stick.

2007/8: a significant change in common with the outdoor rules was the move to a two-year cycle for the production and publication of the rules of indoor hockey.

Specific changes included:

— permitting a team either to have a goalkeeper on the field (with full protective equipment or only with protective headgear) or to play entirely with field players (in which case no player has goalkeeping privileges).

— specifying the face protection which field players are permitted to wear especially in relation to defending a penalty corner.

— clarifying that a defender must not be penalised if their stick is not motionless or is travelling towards the ball while attempting to stop or deflect the shot even when the ball is above shoulder height.

— permitting a goalkeeper to use their hands, arms or any other part of their body (and not just their stick, kickers and leg-guards as hitherto) to move the ball away but only as part of a goal saving action and not to propel the ball forcefully so that it travels a long distance.

Rules Decision Making

The history of the process by which decisions about the Rules of Hockey have been made.

Hockey Rules Board in1900

The Hockey Rules Board (HRB) was founded in 1900 as the International Rules Board (IRB). From 1902 it comprised representatives of the men's Associations of England, Ireland, Scotland and Wales appointed by their respective associations. The Hockey Association (England) had more representatives and also held the chairmanship under a formal constitution of 1909.

IRB 1908

The first reference to the publication of the Rules of the Game appears in the minutes of the IRB 1908, where the minute refers to the publication of the 24th edition of the rules. Whether this publication was in the form of a rule book is not stated but rule books were published in the 1930s and published annually from the late 1940s.

From 1909 the IRB decided to deal with all aspects of hockey including the Rules of the Game and changed its name to the International Hockey Board (IHB).

Rules in Women's Game

Women players used the men's rules until the late 1930's when the All England Women's Hockey Association (AEWHA, the women's hockey world leader) made a few alterations. After 1945 the women's rules deviated further from the men's rules and the women's Associations in membership of the women only International Federation of Women's Hockey Associations (IFWHA) used rules published by the AEWHA.

Discussions and contacts were, however, being made by the IHB and representatives of the IFWHA. There was the anomalous position that women hockey players, playing under the authority of the FIH, were using rules of the game formulated by the IHB whilst those women players who were solely playing under the aegis of the IFWHA were using several different rules of the game. In 1956 the FIH agreed to allow their women players to play to IFWHA rules for international matches.

Rules in 1948

The International Hockey Federation (FIH) was invited to send three representatives to IHB meetings which number was increased to four in 1957.

Rules in 1966

The Board formulated a new Constitution (revised in 1968) which provided for eight representatives from the FIH, four from England and two each from Ireland, Scotland and Wales (all men). Its name was changed to the International Hockey Rules Board (IHRB) and now concentrated solely on the rules of the game.

Rules in 1968

The IFWHA set up its own Rules Board (the WIHRB) but the IHRB met with the WIHRB in that year and agreed to work towards eventually producing rules for both men and women. However, for some time there remained differences between the men's and women's rules regarding substitutes, free hits and the weight of the stick but within a few years all were resolved to provide a definitive set of rules.

Rules in 1972

The IHRB dissolved itself in 1971 and from 1972 appointments to the Board were made by the Council of the FIH. In the new constitution approved by the FIH Council it was clearly stated that the Board would be solely responsible for all Rules of the Game and of requirements on hockey equipment.

It was also decreed that the Board was to be an independent body within the FIH. A new Board (still all men) was duly appointed by the FIH, comprising 10 members, a Chairman and an Honorary Secretary. In recognition of the role of England in rule-making, the FIH appointed an English Chairman.

Between 1972 and 1975 negotiations between the FIH, the IFWHA, the WIHRB and the IHRB continued including a special meeting held in Amsterdam in 1973. The most significant event was the defining meeting between representatives of the FIH and IFWHA in Edinburgh in 1975 which agreed there should be only one Board controlling the Rules of the Game. Even after the combined rule book of 1975 was published under the authority of the two Boards, there were still a few problems to overcome.

In 1973 the Board met for the first time outside London in Amsterdam followed by a first meeting outside Europe in Buenos Aires in 1978.

Rule in 1980's

The remaining problems were settled in time for a new Board, entitled the Hockey Rules Board (HRB), to meet on 9 February 1980. This Board, the combined one as earlier envisaged, comprised 14 members (seven men and seven women, including a Chairman and Hon Secretary), with the Chairmanship going to Mrs Doris Crisp of the IFWHA and AEWHA. The meeting was opened by the respective Presidents of the FIH and IFWHA, Mr R Frank and Mrs E Hyndman. Three years later the two international bodies merged as one FIH. Some years later the FIH abandoned equal representation for men and women on the Board but ensured in appointments that both genders were represented.

The latter half of the twentieth century also saw many changes in equipment. For at least the first fifty years, hockey sticks were solely made from wood, hockey balls were leather cricket balls painted white and goalkeepers used cricket (batsmen's) leg-guards.

Equipment in this original fashion (plus the adoption of shin-guards) continued until the 1950s when gradually other materials (plastic coatings and synthetic materials) appeared on sticks and balls were made of non-traditional materials.

In the early 1980s protective specialist equipment for goalkeepers became the norm, including headgear and overall body padding. Prior to these innovations goalkeepers were usually only equipped with leg-guards, gloves and soccer boots as kickers.

Rule in1994

On 23 April 1994, the FIH Council approved a new Constitution for the HRB and confirmed that the Board was solely responsible for final decisions on all matters in connection with the making, interpreting and altering of the rules of hockey and including requirements covering all equipment used in the game with the power also to prohibit the use of certain items of equipment.

Rule in 1995

In 1995, a Rules Advisory Panel (RAP) was appointed by the FIH to assist the HRB in considering new rules, trials and experiments.

Rule in 1998

The Statutes of the FIH, approved by the 1998 FIH Congress, listed the HRB as having separate status from other FIH Committees with its own constitution. However, in November 1998 the FIH Council decided to remove this complete autonomy of the HRB. The decisions of the HRB on the rules of the game (outdoor and indoor) were to be subject to the approval or rejection (but not amendment) of the FIH Council before implementation. In October 1999 the FIH confirmed that

RAP would act as an advisory body reporting to the HRB and that the HRB had explicit responsibility for "all matters in connection with making, interpreting and altering the rules of hockey and guidance thereon".

Rule in 2001

With effect from 2001 when revised Statutes were adopted by the FIH, the HRB was further subsumed into the FIH structure. The RAP was disbanded and responsibility for development of the rules including conducting trials was made a specific and direct responsibility of the HRB. The membership of the HRB was revised and included more members with extensive playing, coaching and team management responsibilities in recognition of this wider remit. The HRB retains its title and modus operandi but is now effectively one of the committees reporting to the Executive Board of the FIH.

This *History of Rules Decision Making* is based on a *Chronology of the Rules of Hockey* researched and produced on behalf of the Hockey Rules Board by Ernest Wall, Evlyn Raistrick and George Croft in 2000 to mark the centenary of the establishment of the International Rules Board which subsequently became the Hockey Rules Board.

13

Hockey in India

Despite being anointed India's national game, hockey lags far behind cricket and other games in the popularity stakes. When Indian sportspersons are rapidly asserting themselves in the world stage, India's hockey fortune is plummeting to an abyss in the international fora.

During the heydays of Indian hockey, the national team called the shots in major sporting events, annihilating opponents with utter disdain. But gradually things took a turn for the worse with the Indian team failing to keep pace with vastly improving European rivals. With success being far and few between, hockey is losing out to other popular sports that have brought India international success.

History

Even though many ancient civilizations played hockey in different variations, the modern game of hockey—the field hockey-evolved in the British Isles in the 19th century.

Hockey was introduced in India by British Army regiments and the game soon found favour among the native Indians. The first hockey club in India came up in Calcutta in 1885-86 and soon Bombay and Punjab followed suit.

Making its Olympic debut at the 1928 Amsterdam Games, Indian hockey team cruised home to its first Olympic gold without conceding a single goal. The hallmark of this ruthless domination was the wizardry of Indian hockey legend Dhyan Chand who mesmerized the Amsterdam crowd with his dazzling skills.

From 1928 to 1956, the Indian hockey juggernaut won six straight Olympic gold medals while winning 24 consecutive matches. This was the golden era of Indian hockey when India loomed large in world hockey and produced some of the finest players the game has ever seen.

The Indian stranglehold over the Olympic hockey gold came to an end when Pakistan defeated India in the final of the 1960 Rome Olympics.

— The Indian Hockey Federation was formed at Gwalior in 1925. India joined the International Hockey Federation (FIH) in 1928, becoming the first non-European member of the FIH.

— The first Indian sports teams to ever set foot in Australia/New Zealand (1926), Europe (1928) and Japan/USA (1932) were the Indian hockey teams. The first Indian sports team to do a round-the-world tour was the 1932 Indian hockey team. They played matches in Colombo, Malaya, Tokyo, Los Angeles, Omaha, Philadelphia, Amsterdam, Berlin, Prague and Budapest, before triumphantly returning to the shores of India.

— Asia's first Olympic gold medal was won by the 1928 Indian Olympic hockey team. After the 1928 Amsterdam Olympics, an awe-struck Dutch journalist wrote *"The Indian ball seems ignorant of the laws of gravity. One of those tanned diabolical jugglers stares at the ball intently; it gets upright and remains suspended in the air. This is no longer the game of hockey. It is a juggling turn. It is splendid."*

— After the 1932 Olympics, the Los Angeles sports journalists voted the Indian hockey team's showing as *"the most outstanding exhibition of skill in any sport in the Olympics."* A cartoon published in the Evening News of India showed Dhyan Chand's stick in the form of a cobra, and Dhyan Chand whistling in front of it like a snake charmer. The Viceroy of India sent a cable congratulating the Olympic champions. It read, *"I am delighted to learn of the splendid victory of our hockey team. Please give all members of the side my warm congratulations upon retaining the world championship."*

— In the 1936 Berlin Olympics, Dhyan Chand, who was the captain of the team, had the distinction of scoring 11 out of 38 goals scored by his side. The Fuhrer was very impressed by Dhyan Chand's performance in the final, where India whipped Germany 8-1 in front of 40,000 fans. At a dinner party after the final, Hitler offered to elevate Dhyan Chand to the rank of a Colonel if he migrated to Germany. Ever the patriot, Dhyan Chand turned down the offer.

— Dhyan Chand was to hockey what Bradman is to cricket and Pele is to football. Dhyan Chand scored over a thousand goals in a career spanning 1926-1948. The ultimate tribute was paid to him by a sports club in Vienna, which built a statue of Dhyan Chand with four hands and four sticks. To those Viennese, no ordinary man with two hands and one stick could have played so well.

— The first sporting achievement of independent India was the 1948 Olympic hockey gold medal. Over 25,000 spectators watched the 1948 Olympic hockey final between India and Britain, played at Wembley. This was the first time that India and Britain played an official hockey match, and India went on to beat Britain 4-0. That was the first time that India's national flag was displayed and India's national anthem, *Jana Gaṇa Mana*, was played at an Olympic venue.

— England introduced both cricket and hockey to India. While it took 20 years and 15 matches before India beat England in cricket for the first time (1952 test in Chennai), it took 37 years and 22 matches before England beat India in hockey for the first time (Britain 2 - India 1, 1985 Champions Trophy in Perth). As long as England ruled India, they never played a match with the Indian hockey team.

— India has won a grand total of 8 Olympic gold medals in hockey – in no other sport has India won even an Olympic silver medal, let alone the gold. India holds the records for the largest victory margin in an Olympic final (India 8 - Germany 1 in the 1936 Olympic final), the largest victory margin in a pool match (India 24 - USA 1 in the 1932 Olympics), and the largest number of consecutive victories (30 wins on the trot from 1928 to 1960).

— So dominant was the Indian hockey team of old that it took 28 years for India to score only 1 goal in a match (India 1 - Germany 0 in the 1956 Olympic semi-final), and it took 40 years before a country scored more than one goal against India in the Olympics (New Zealand 2 - India 1 in the 1968 Olympics).

— In men's hockey, India are currently title-holders of the Junior Asia Cup (2004), Asia Cup (2003), Afro-Asian Games (2003), Junior World Cup (2001) and the Sub-Junior Asia Cup (2001). In women's hockey,

India are currently title-holders of the Asia Cup (2004), Afro-Asian Games (2003), Commonwealth Games (2002) and the Sub-Junior Asia Cup (2000).

— Sansarpur, a tiny village on the outskirts of Jalandhar, has the distinction of producing 9 Olympians - Gurmit Singh (1932), Udham Singh (1952, '56, '60, '64), Gurdev Singh (1956), Darshan Singh (1964), Jagjit Singh (1964, '68), Balbir Singh—Services, Balbir Singh—Punjab and Tarsem Singh (1968), and the World Cup winning captain Ajitpal Singh (1968, '72, '76).

— The most common surname among Indian hockey players is Singh. As a foreign journalist wrote in his dispatch, "Singh initiated the move. After dodging past a defender, Singh passed the ball to Singh, who centered it to Singh and Singh scored the goal with a reverse flick."

— Within the community of Singhs, the name Balbir has a glorious record in Indian hockey. Six Balbir Singhs did duty for India—Balbir Singh (Sr.), Balbir Singh (Jr.), Balbir Singh (Punjab), Balbir Singh (Services), Balbir Singh (Railways) and Balbir Singh (Navy). Between them, they represented India in 5 Olympic Games (winning 4 Golds and 3 Bronzes) and 2 Asian Games (winning 3 Golds and 2 Silvers).

— Kodagu (mispronounced as Coorg by the British) is the hockey hotbed of Karnataka. It hosts the annual Kodava Hockey Festival, the largest family sports tournament in the world. Every year, the tournament takes on a different name and is held in a different town, based on the family that is organizing it. Each team is made up of members of only one, blood-related family. Women can also participate; they have the choice of representing either their paternal side or maternal side. The 2003 tournament saw the participation of 281 family teams.

— 5 pairs of brothers have done duty for India in the Olympics. The most famous pair was that of Dhyan Chand (1928, '32, '36) and Roop Singh (1932, '36). Of the remaining four pairs, 2 pairs played for India in the same Olympics—Balbir Singh (Railways) and Gurbux Singh (1968), and Harmeek Singh (1968, '72) and Ajit Singh (1972, '76). The pair of brothers to represent India over separate Olympics are V. J. Peters (1960, '64, '68) and V. J. Philips (1972, '76), and Vivek Singh (1992) and Rahul Singh (1996).

— Father-son pairs to have represented India include Dhyan Chand—Ashok Kumar, Ahmad Sher Khan—Aslam Sher Khan, Leslie Claudius—Robert Claudius and Ajeet Singh - Gagan Ajeet Singh.

— India has not done very well in the elite Champions Trophy. In the 25 times that this event has been held, India has qualified for this premier event only 9 times, has never won the title, and has finished last twice. India has lost more than 50% of its matches played in the Champions Trophy.

— India's best come-from-behind performance was in the 1985 Champions Trophy, in their match against Germany at Perth. India were trailing 1-5. Pargat Singh rose to the ocassion with two goals, including a solo goal starting right from the Indian defence. Still trailing 4-5, India managed to score a goal with only 20 seconds left, to snatch a thrilling 5-5 draw.

Golden Moments

Hockey is the only event in which India has won Gold Medals—8 of them. Hockey was considered the National Game of India. Unmatched excellence and incomparable virtuosity brought India a string of Olympic gold medals. The brilliant Indians brought a touch of black magic to their play and the ball juggling feats of the Indians were a sheer delight.

The Golden Era of hockey in India was the period from 1928—1956 when India won 6 consecutive gold medals in the Olympics. During the Golden Era, India played 24 Olympic matches, won all 24, scored 178 goals (at an average of 7.43 goals per match) and conceded only 7 goals. The two other gold medals for India came in the 1964 Tokyo Olympics and the 1980 Moscow Olympics.

In 1956, after India won the last of its six consecutive gold medals, the manager of the Pakistan hockey team, Riazuddin Ahmed said, "This is the first time that we played India in the Olympics. The next time we play, the result will be different." His prophetic words came true in 1960, when after 28 consecutive victories in the Olympic Games, India lost 0-1 to Pakistan in the 1960 Rome Olympics final. Gold had finally turned to silver and a magical era had ended. The pages that follow recreate the glory of India's golden moments in the Olympics. Enjoy!

Snippets from the Indian freedom struggle will be the lead-ins to the main text. Our Golden Era in the Olympics also coincided with important moments in India's history like the Non-Cooperation, Civil Disobedience and Quit India Movements, Dandi Yatra, Round Table Conferences, and the Azad Hind Fauj.

190 years after Robert Clive lead a band of 800 Englishmen and 2220 Indian mercenaries to victory over Nawab Siraj-ud-daula's army of 50,000 troops at Plassey, 90 years after Mangal Pandey triggered off the first Indian War of Independence, India attained her freedom at the stroke of the midnight hour on August 15, 1947. We have chosen as our theme martyrs who died for the freedom of their beloved country.

Indian Hockey Federation

The All India Hockey Federation was formed in 1925 with Colonel Bruce Turnbull as President and M. S. Ansari as Secretary. The Federation held its first National Championships at Calcutta in 1928.

The IHF seeks to promote, encourage and develop the game of hockey in India and holds a number of inter-member tournaments and National Championship Tournaments.

India national field hockey team

The **Indian hockey team** is the national field hockey team of India. The team was formed in 1928, when the Indian Hockey Federation was formed in Gwalior and was the first non-European team to be a part of the International Hockey Federation. The team was the first ever international Indian team to set foot in Australia and New Zealand (1926). In 1928, the team won their first Olympic gold medal.

From 1928 to 1956, India remained unbeaten in the Olympics garnering six gold medals in a row. Today the Indian team has won a total of eight gold, one silver and two bronze medals in Olympics.

In recent times, the Indian team, while possessing some of finest stick-wielders in the world, have had a tendency to choke on the big occasions. At tournaments like the 2004 Olympics, 2005 Men's Champions Trophy (which was on home soil) and the 2006 Men's Hockey World Cup the team has shown an inability to gel and has finished in positions well below their talent (in a similar vein to the Spanish national football team).

Premier Hockey League India

The Premier Hockey League (PHL) is a joint project of

ESPN-Star Sports, Indian Hockey Federation (IHF) and Leisure Sports Management and is modelled on the U.S. NBA league. The PHL was conceived to give a shot in the arm to the domestic hockey scenario and revive sagging interest in the game of hockey.

The inaugural edition of the PHL kicked-off at the Gachibowli Stadium, Hyderabad, on January 13, 2005. The PHL is made up of ten teams divided into two tiers, the Premier Division and the First Division. The league follows a round-robin format with all teams playing each other twice.

The PHL incorporates a slew of innovations to make the games more exciting and spectator friendly. The participating teams sport fancy names and boast of foreign players in their ranks. Instead of normal 70-minute hockey games with two sessions, the PHL games have four sessions each of 17.5 minutes. Teams can take time-outs to chalk out new strategies to deal with emerging situations.

The PHL will be telecast live by ESPN-STAR Sports for the next ten years. The company employs twelve television cameras to cover all possible angles and the matches begin at eight in the evening to maximize television viewer ship.

The 2005 edition was won by the Hyderabad Sultans while in 2006, Bangalore Lions defeated Chandigarh Dynamos to emerge victorious.

Hockey Stadiums in India

The hockey stadiums in India are equipped with synthetic turfs and spectator friendly amenities. Over the years, they have played host to many memorable contests.

Here is a list of major hockey grounds in India: Mayor Radhakrishnan Stadium, Egmore, Chennai:

Radhakrishnan Stadium is regarded by the International Hockey Federation as one of the best in the world for its state-of-the-art infrastructure. After installation of a synthetic turf surface in 1995, the stadium hosted the hockey event in the SAF Games and the 1996 Champions Trophy

In 2004, the stadium was redesigned and upgraded by the Sports Authority of Tamil Nadu to prepare the venue for hosting the 2005 Champions Trophy in December. After the renovation drive, the stadium features a re-laid synthetic hockey surface and floodlights of international standards.

Major Dhyan Chand National Stadium, Delhi: The erstwhile National Stadium, known as the "temple of Indian hockey," was dedicated to the memory of Indian hockey legend Major Dhyan Chand in 2002. The Stadium boasts of two brand new synthetic hockey turfs and has a capacity of 25,000. In preparation for the 2010 Delhi Commonwealth Games, the hockey pitches will be equipped with floodlights and electronic and video-matrix scoreboard.

Gachibowli Stadium, Hyderabad: The Gachibowli Stadium was built by construction major Larsen & Toubro Ltd. in mere 70 days for the 2003 SAF Games. This state-of-the-art stadium hosted the 2005 Premier Hockey League.

K. D. Singh Babu Stadium, Lucknow: The stadium was named in the memory of famous Indian hockey player Kunwar Digvijay Singh "Babu."

Surjeet Hockey Stadium, Jalandhar: This astro-turf stadium was named after Olympian Surjeet Singh.

Hockey Tournaments in India

The Indian hockey tournaments are played throughout the year and are conducted under the aegis of the Indian Hockey federation. Here is a list of major hockey competitions in India:

- — All India MCC Murugappa Gold Cup Hockey Tournament
- — All India Aagha Khan Hockey Tournament
- — All India Lal Bahadur Shastri Hockey Tournament
- — All India Beighton Cup Hockey Tournament
- — Obaidullah Khan Gold Cup

Women field Hockey in India

Indian women's hockey has played a very important role in Asia, but it has failed to make presence in world cup and Olympic games like it's male counterparts.

India has never qualified in an Olympic games and in world cup, its best result was 4th position in year 1974 in the 1st women's world cup hockey held in France. From 1974 til 2002 India failed to qualify for the Women's World Cup. At the 2002 Women's World Cup, India places 12th and in 2006, India places 11th.

India has been home to some of the most outstanding hockey players the game has ever seen. From the legendary Dhyan Chand to the inspirational Dhanraj Pillay, Indian hockey players have delighted hockey connoisseurs around the world.

Here is a list of some famous Indian hockey players:

Dhyan Chand

Achievements:

Arguably the greatest player the game of hockey has ever produced, Dhyan Chand's genius transcended national boundaries and created myths abound of his phenomenal abilities. Once a lowly sepoy in the British Indian Army, Dhyan Chand's wizardry with the hockey stick caught the attention of his seniors and soon earned him a place in the Indian national team. Representing India in three Olympics, Dhyan Chand mesmerized the world audience with his audacious jugglery and leadership qualities.

At the 1932 Los Angeles Olympics, when India thrashed the U. S. by 24 goals to one, Dhyan Chand and his brother Roop Singh wreaked havoc in the opposition defence, each scoring eight goals. Four years later, at the Berlin Games, Dhyan Chand was again in the thick of action when India drubbed the hosts by a huge margin in the final.

Such was Dhyan Chand's virtuosity that people actually refused to believe what they have seen with their naked eyes. They broke his stick in Holland to check if there was a magnet inside and in Japan they decided it was glue. In Vienna Sports Club, there stands a statue of Dhyan Chand with four hands and four sticks.

Dhyan Chand was conferred the Padma Bhushan, India's third highest civilian award, in 1956. The 'National Sports Day' in India is observed on his birthday

Leslie Claudius

Figured in the Guinness Book of World Records for maximum number of Olympic medals in hockey (3 gold and 1 silver); Padma Shri in 1971

Leslie Claudius stands tall among a bevy of Indian hockey legends. Born on March 25, 1927, Claudius was hailed as one of the finest right-halves of his time.

For someone who started with football and even played in the IFA Shield, Leslie's rise in the Indian hockey turf was meteoric. An ace right-half with great distribution and tackling skills, Leslie virtually owned that position in the world-beating Indian team that won three consecutive Olympic gold medals from 1948 to 1956.

Balbir Singh Sr.

Won three gold medals teams in the 1948, 1952 and 1956 Olympic Games; silver medal at the Asian Games 1958 as well as the Asian Games 1962; first hockey player to be awarded the Padma Shri

Balbir Singh Sr., born on October 10, 1924, was one of the best centre-forwards to have played for India. An opportunist in the penalty circle, Balbir was bestowed with the uncanny knack to score goals at will.

Balbir was a member of the gold winning Indian hockey teams in the 1948, 1952 and 1956 Olympic Games. He was the flag bearer of the Indian Olympic Contingent at the 1952 Helsinki Olympics and 1956 Melbourne Olympics. Balbir was also a member of the Indian hockey team that won the silver medal at the Asian Games 1958 as well as the Asian Games 1962.

Post-retirement, Balbir enjoyed a successful stint as Indian team manager leading the team to a silver medal in the 1971 World Cup and the gold in the 1975 World Cup. In 1957, Balbir Singh Senior became the first hockey player to be awarded the Padma Shri.

Ajit Pal Singh

Asian All-Star team member in 1974; captain of the World Cup winning Indian team in 1975

Ajit Pal Singh was an outstanding centre-half of Indian hockey team. Born on April 1, 1947, Ajit Pal hailed from Punjab's Sansarpur village, the hotbed of a generation of legendary Indian hockey players.

Ajit Pal Singh made his international debut in 1966 and the next year he took part in the Pre-Olympic tournament in London and booked his place in the Indian team for the 1968 Mexico Olympics. Despite Indian finishing third, Ajitpal made a fine impression with his precise and flawless ball distribution. He captained the Indian team that played the 1976 Olympics in Montreal.

Ajit Pal represented India at the 1970 Bangkok Asian Games and captained the team to the 1974 Teheran Asian Games, India emerging second best each time. Ajit's dexterous display earned him a place in the Asian All-Star team in 1974.

The watermark of Ajit Pal Singh's illustrious career was the 1975 World Cup when he led India to their maiden Cup victory with an emphatic win over archrivals Pakistan. The whole country reveled in this magnificent triumph and the victorious team received a rousing welcome.

Udham Singh

After Leslie Claudius only hockey player to win 3 gold and one silver in Olympic Games; Arjuna Award in 1965

Udham Singh is undoubtedly one of the finest hockey players to have donned the India colours. Udham Singh was born on August 4, 1928, in the hockey bastion of Sansarpur in Punjab.

After being picked up to play for a strong Punjab Police team boasting a number of Olympians, Udham Singh missed the 1948 Olympics due to a nagging finger injury. He was a mainstay of the formidable Indian team that won consecutive gold medals in the 1952 Helsinki and 1956 Melbourne.

Udham Singh made his farewell Olympic appearance in the 1964 Tokyo Games when India avenged their previous Olympic final loss to Pakistan to emerge the winners.

Udham Singh coached the Indian team that won Silver at the 1967 Olympics in London and 1970 Asian Games in Bangkok. In recognition to his services to the nation, Udham Singh was conferred the Arjuna Award.

K. D. Singh Babu

Won gold medals in 1948 and 1952 Olympics; Padma Shri in 1960. Kunwar Digvijay Singh, popularly knows as K. D. Singh Babu, was born on February 2, 1923, at Bara Banki in Uttar Pradesh. Digvijay's peers in the Indian hockey team fondly called him "Babu" for the touch of aristocracy he lent in everything he did.

After getting into the national team, K. D. Singh toured British East Africa (Kenya), Uganda, and Tanzania in 1947 with the Indian hockey team captained by hockey maestro Dhyan Chand and established his reputation as a prolific goal-scorer.

K. D. Singh Babu was the vice-captain of the Indian team that won the gold medal at the 1948 London Olympics, the first Olympic hockey gold for independent India. He led the Indian team to another gold medal at the 1952 Helsinki Olympics.

In 1960, Kunwar Digvijay Singh was honoured with the Padma Shri award, thereby becoming the second Padma Shri hockey player after Balbir Singh Sr.

Mohammed Shahid

Best Forward of 1980 Champions Trophy; gold medal in 1980 Moscow Olympic Games; member of Asian All-Star team in 1986; Arjuna Award in 1980-81; Padma Shri in 1986

Mohammed Shahid ranks as one of the finest Indian forwards ever. Shahid was born on April 14, 1960, at Varanasi in Uttar Pradesh.

Shahid made his international debut in the Junior World Cup in France in 1979 and immediately made a mark for his excellent dribbling and ball-control skills. After graduating to the seniors team, Mohammad Shahid represented India at the Champions Trophy at Karachi in

1980. Despite Indian team's listless display, Shahid was adjudged the Best Forward of the tournament.

Shahid was a member of the gold medal-winning Indian team at the 1980 Olympic Games in Moscow. He also represented India in the 1984 Olympics in Los Angeles and the 1988 Olympics in Seoul. Shahid was in the team that won silver medal at the 1982 Asian Games in Delhi and Bronze at the 1986 Asian Games in Seoul. Shahid's sublime skills at the 1986 Asian Games earned him a place in the Asian All-Star team.

Master dribbler who mesmerized fans with his virtuosity, Shahid was awarded the Arjuna Award in 1980-81 and Padma Shri in 1986.

Dhanraj Pillay

sHighest goal scorer in the Bangkok Asian Games; member of World Eleven side during the 1994 World Cup; Padma Shri in 2000; Rajiv Gandhi Khel Ratna Award (1999).

Dhanraj Pillay, ace Indian striker, was born on July 16, 1968 at Kirkee in Maharashtra. The hero of many epic Indian victories, the mercurial Dhanraj has been to Indian hockey what Leander Paes has been to Indian tennis.

Dhanraj fine-tuned his raw talent under the tutelage of elder brother Ramesh, who himself was a former India international. After a fine stint with his employers Mahindra & Mahindra and Mumbai in national championships, Dhanraj was called for India duty in the Asia Cup of 1989.

In a glorious career spanning 15 years, Dhanraj has represented India in four Summer Olympics ('92, '96, 2000, 2004), four World Hockey Cups, four Champions Trophies, four Asian Games, and four Asia Cups. For a long time, Dhanraj has been synonymous with Indian hockey and his spirited efforts have kept the Indian tricolour flying high in more occasions than one.

Dhanraj was the highest goal scorer in the Bangkok Asian Games and was the only Indian player to figure in the World Eleven side during the 1994 World Cup at Sydney.

The nation has profusely rewarded Dhanraj Pillay for his relentless pursuit for excellence and his unflinching commitment to the Indian cause. He has received the prestigious Rajiv Gandhi Khel Ratna Award (1999) and been conferred with the coveted Padma Shri in 2000.

Gagan Ajit Singh

Captain of the Indian junior team that won Junior World Cup in 2001; member of the All-Asian men's hockey team in 2002; Arjuna Award in 2003

Gagan Ajit Singh is one of the mainstays of the present Indian hockey team. Born on December 9, 1980, at Ferozepore, Punjab, Gagan Ajit developed a passion for the game at an early age since both his father, Ajit Singh, and uncle, Harmik Singh, were former Olympians of repute.

A fleet-footed centre-forward, Gagan Ajit made his first impression on the national circuit scoring a record 27 goals in the 1997 Junior Nationals for the Air-India Academy. Carrying on the good work, he also emerged as the highest scorer for Air-India in the all-India Gurmit Singh tournament and the Jawaharlal Nehru tournament in 1997.

Riding on this goal-spree Gagan earned his place in the national team and promptly announced his arrival at the big stage by scoring in his debut match against Trinidad & Tobago at the 1998 Commonwealth Games in

Kuala Lumpur. Since then Gagan Ajeet has become a regular feature in the Indian frontline.

In 2001, Gagan Ajit led the Indian junior squad to a fabulous triumph at the Junior World Cup held at Hobart, Australia. Gagan was named in the All-Asian men's hockey team in 2002 after the 14th Asian Games held in Busan, South Korea.

14

Hockey Tournaments

Field hockey (also referred to as simply *hockey*) was introduced at the Summer Olympic Games as a men's competition at the 1908 Games in London, with six teams, including four from the United Kingdom of Great Britain and Ireland. Hockey was removed from the Olympics at the 1924 Paris Games due to the lack of an international structure. The International Hockey Federation (FIH, *Fédération Internationale de Hockey*) was founded in Paris that year as a response to hockey's omission. Men's hockey became a permanent fixture at the next Olympic Games, the 1928 Games in Amsterdam.

The first women's Olympic hockey competition was at the 1980 Moscow Games. Olympic field hockey games were first played on artificial turf at the 1976 Montreal Games.

Hockey World Cup

The Hockey World Cup, sometimes called the Hockey World Championships, is an international field hockey competition organised by the International Hockey Federation (FIH). The tournament was started in 1971. It is held every four years, bridging the four years between the Summer Olympics.

There is also a Women's Hockey World Cup, which has been held since 1974 and was organised by the International Federation of Women's Hockey Associations (IFWHA) until 1981, when the governing bodies merged into the current International Hockey Federation.

Five countries have dominated the event's history. Pakistan is the most successful team, having won the tournament four times. The Netherlands have won three titles, and Germany has won two titles. India and Australia have each won the tournament once.

The 2006 Hockey World Cup was held at the Warsteiner HockeyPark, Mönchengladbach, Germany from September 6 to September 17. Germany won for the second time, defeating Australia 4–3 in the final. The FIH decided to allot the next Hockey World Cup in 2010 to India.

History

The Hockey World Cup was first conceived by Pakistan's Air Marshal Nur Khan and India's Jimmy Nagarwalla. They proposed their idea to the FIH under the name of Patrick Rowley, the first editor of *World Hockey* magazine. Their idea was approved on October 26, 1969, and adopted by the FIH Council at a meeting in Brussels on April 12, 1970. The FIH decided that the inaugural World Cup would be held in October 1971, in Pakistan.

However, political issues would prevent that first competition from being played in Pakistan. Pakistan and India had been at war with each other only six years earlier.

When Pakistan invited India to compete in the tournament, a crisis arose. Pakistanis, led by cricketer Abdul Hafeez Kardar, protested against India's participation in the Hockey World Cup, threatening to burn down the stadium if the country's team was allowed to play. Meanwhile, they hijacked an Indian Airlines Fokker Friendship aircraft to Lahore Airport, where they set the plane on fire. In turn, Pakistan threatened that they would not participate if India hosted the tournament.

In 1971, there was also a civil war between West Pakistan and East Pakistan, now known as the Bangladesh Liberation War. This led to political instability throughout the country. Given the intense political climate between Pakistan and India, the FIH decided to move the tournament elsewhere. In March 1971, the FIH decided to move the first Hockey World Cup to the Real Club de Polo grounds in Barcelona, Spain, which was considered a neutral and peaceful European site.

The FIH has set no requirements or limitations on the size of the competition. The 1971 Cup included only ten nations, the smallest World Cup to date. The 1978 Cup featured fourteen nations. The 2002 Cup featured sixteen nations, the largest World Cup to date.

The first three tournaments were held every two years. The 1978 Cup was the only tournament held three years from the previous tournament. Since 1982, the tournament has been held every four years, halfway between the Summer Olympics field hockey competition.

History

The Hockey World Cup trophy was designed by the Bashir Moojid and created by the Pakistani Army. On March 27, 1971, in Brussels, the trophy was formally handed to FIH President Rene Frank by Mr H.E Masood, the Pakistani Ambassador to Belgium. The trophy consists of a silver cup with an intricate floral design, surmounted by a globe of the world in silver and gold, placed on a high blade base inlaid with ivory. At its peak is a model hockey stick and ball. Without its base, the trophy stands 120.85 mm high. Including the base, the trophy stands 650 mm. It weighs 11,560 g, including 895 g of gold, 6815 g of silver, 350 g of ivory and 3500 g of teak wood.

Qualification

The qualification stage has been a part of the Hockey World Cup since 1977. All participating teams play in the qualification round. The teams divide into two or more pools and compete for a berth in the final tournament. The top two teams are automatically qualified and the rest of the berths are decided in playoffs

Features

The final tournament features the continental champions and other qualified teams. Sometimes it also features the winners of the Summer Olympics' hockey competition or the continental runners-up. The teams divide into pools once more and play a round robin tournament. The composition of the pools is determined using the current world rankings.

The top two teams in each pool play in the semifinals for a place in the final. The bottom two teams in the semifinals have a third place playoff. The rest of the teams have playoffs to determine their final positions. If they are third or fourth in their pool, they play for fifth place; if they are fifth or sixth in their pool, they play for ninth place.

Hockey Champions Trophy

Hockey Champions Trophy the Hockey Champions Trophy is the International Hockey Federation's most prestigious annual event (since 1980). Founded by the

Pakistan Air Marshal Nur Khan, it features the world's top-ranked teams competing in a round robin format. The Pakistan Hockey Federation started the competition as a men's tournament in 1978 and it was only as late as 1987 that the first women's tournament took place.

The tournament became an annual affair after 1980. Australia, the Netherlands and Germany (including West Germany before reunification) have all won the trophy a record eight times. Pakistan is the only Asian champion in 1980. Six teams qualify for the championship, though the first edition had five teams, the second had seven and 1987 had eight. In the year following the Olympics or a World Cup, the six teams include the host, the defending champion, the world champion and the next highest ranked teams from either the most recent World Cup or Olympic Games.

The last placed team in the tournament is dropped and replaced by the winner of the Champions Challenge, which was introduced in 2001 and can be considered as the Champions Trophy for so called B-nations. The 2007 Women's Champions Trophy was held from January 13 to January 21, 2007 in Quilmes, Argentina. The 2007 Men's Champions Trophy will be held from December 1 to December 9, 2007 in Lahore, Pakistan.

Sultan Azlan Shah Cup

The Sultan Azlan Shah Cup is an annual field hockey tournament held in Malaysia. It began in 1983 as a biennial contest. The tournament became an annual event after 1998, following its growth and popularity. The tournament is named after the ninth Yang di-Pertuan Agong (King) of Malaysia, Sultan Azlan Shah, an avid fan of field hockey.

15th Sultan Azlan Shah Cup, 2006

The 15th Azlan Shah Hockey Tournament started in Kuala Lumpur, Malaysia on Sunday June 18, 2006. This year, the tournament is divided into two pools. The top two teams after the round robin matches in each pool will clash in the semi finals of the tournament.

Four times Sultan Azlan Shah Cup holder, Australia is playing as the defending champion from last year when they defeated Pakistan 4-3 in the Finals. They also won the Cup in 2004. Asian Champions India, winners of the Azlan Shah in 1991 and 1995, are looking to overcome a series of disappointments in the international arena over the last two years while Pakistan was only able to win this cup in 2000.

Hockey Champions Challenge

The Hockey Champions Challenge is an international field hockey tournament, played every two years. It was introduced in 2001 by the International Hockey Federation (FIH) in order to broaden hockey's competitive base at world level.

The tournament traditionally features the teams ranked seventh to twelfth in the world as determined by finishes in the most recent Olympic Games (and Olympic Qualifying Tournament) or World Cup (and World Cup Qualifier). In addition to an automatic spot for the host nation, the tournament field also includes the team ranked sixth and last at the previous Champions Trophy.

The Champions Challenge can be considered as the Champions Trophy for the so called *B-nations*. The winner of the event will participate in the Champions Trophy in the following year.

Women's Champions Trophy (field hockey)

The Women's Champions Trophy is an annual field

hockey tournament for the world's leading national women's teams. The 2007 edition of the tournament was held in Quilmes, Argentina from January 13 to January 21, 2007.

The seventh match of the 2007 Champions Trophy, the encounter between Spain and Australia on Tuesday January 16 was the 250th match in the Women's CT history. Of the fourteen previous women's Champions Trophies, six have been won by Australia, including an uninterrupted streak from 1991 to 1999. Four editions of the tournament were won by the Netherlands, and one each by South Korea, PR China, Argentina, and Germany.

Teams winning on home soil include the Netherlands in 1987 and 2000, Australia in 1999 and 2003, and China in 2002. The worst finish by a team on home soil was Argentina's sixth place in 1995. Teams which have participated, but never won include Canada, England, Great Britain, New Zealand, South Africa, Spain, United States and Japan.

2007 debutantes Japan are the 14th country to participate in a Champions Trophy. The only other country to have participated only once is Canada with their only appearance in the first edition in 1987. Australia are the only team to have participated in all fifteen editions of the Champions Trophy, with the Netherlands a close second with fourteen participations.

A new joint record was set at the Champions Trophy 2007 in Quilmes with Nadine Ernsting-Krienke (GER) and Magdalena Aicega (ARG) each making their 10th Champions Trophy appearance. When Ernsting-Krienke played her first Champions Trophy in 1991, the youngest player in the current Champions Trophy, Georgina Oliva (ESP) was barely 14 months old.

Of the 108 players in this Champions Trophy, 56 have never played in a CT before. With three players new to hockey's top annual event, the Netherlands have fewest debutantes, while Japan in their first ever CT appearance obviously have most debutantes with all their eighteen players novices to the event.

With three goals in the first five matches of the tournament, Nadine Ernsting-Krienke has overtaken Jackie Pereira as the all-time topscorer for goals scored in Champions Trophy tournaments. Pereira had been the leading scorer with 21 goals, while Ernsting-Krienke is on 22 with one match to go in this event. Ernsting-Krienke however needed ten Champions Trophy editions to achieve this feat while Pereira competed in only five.

The oldest player competing in the this edition was Akemi Kato who turned 36 in December 2006. The youngest player is Georgina Oliva from Spain who will turn 17 next July and is thus not even half Kato's age. The average age of players in this tournament is 24 years and 5 months, with five players 18 years or younger at the start of the event, and eleven players 30 years or older. The oldest team is Japan at an average age of 26 years and 2 months, while Spain are the youngest team at just over 23 years and 4 months.

Format

Each of the six teams plays each other once in a round robin format to complete five preliminary round games. The top two teams at the end of the preliminary round matches play off in the final. The 3rd and 4th placed teams play for the bronze medal, while the 5th and 6th placed teams meet in the 5th place playoff.

If teams are equal on points at the end of the preliminary rounds, they will be ranked according the following criteria (in order):

— Matches won

— Goal difference

— Goals for
— Result between equal teams in preliminary round

If teams can't be separated after the criteria above are applied, then a penalty stroke competition will be played.

2006 Men's Champions Trophy (field hockey)

The 28th edition of the Champions Trophy for men held in Terrassa, Spain from July 22 to July 30, 2006. Six nations participating in this annual elite tournament, they are Argentina, reigning champions Australia, Germany, Pakistan, Netherlands, and hosts Spain. Netherlands emerged tournament champion after beating Germany 2–1 in the final

2006 Women's Hockey World Cup

The 2006 Women's Hockey World Cup is the 11th edition of the Women's Hockey World Cup. It was held from September 27 to October 8, 2006 in Madrid, Spain.

Netherlands won its sixth World Championship after beating Australia 3–1. Defending Champion Argentina finished third after defeating Spain 5–0 in the third place play-off.

2006 Men's Hockey World Cup

The 2006 Hockey World Cup for men is the 11th edition of the Hockey World Cup. It held from September 6 to September 17, 2006 in Mönchengladbach, Germany. Germany won for second consecutive time after beating Australia 4–3 while Spain emerged as third place winner after defeating Korea.

Warsteiner HockeyPark

Warsteiner HockeyPark is a multi-use stadium in

Mönchengladbach, Germany. It is currently used mostly for american football and field hockey matches and hosted the 2006 World Hockey Cup.

The construction started in August 2004, the laying of the foundation stone was in October 2004, the arranging and naming celebration was in April 2005, and the official opening celebration took place on April 15, 2006 in the context of a Four Nation Tournament, featuring Argentina, Germany, India and Spain. The stadium is run by former German field hockey international Michael Hilgers.

Two fields are available and there is one additional field on the backside of the grandstand. The additional field is also equipped with floodlights and a stand for 850 spectators that is made of turf steps. The main field is surrounded by five stands that offer space for more than 9.000 spectators. Mobile stages can be added to increase the number of spectators up to 14.000, which was the case at the Hockey World Cup in 2006, won by the host country Germany.

2005 Men's Champions Trophy (Field Hockey)

The 27st edition of the Men's Champions Trophy took place in the *Mayor Radhakrishnan Stadium* in Chennai, India. Tortured by heavy rain, the event started on Saturday December 10 and ended on Sunday December 18.

Participating nations at the annual men's elite six nations tournament were Australia, hosts India, Germany, Pakistan, The Netherlands, and reigning champions Spain. Olympic champion Australia re-entered the event after a boycott of the 2004 edition. The tournament returned to India after nine years.

Field hockey at the 2004 Summer Olympics

Field Hockey at the 2004 Summer Olympics was held at the Olympic Hockey Centre located within the Helliniko Olympic Complex. There a test competition involving four each men's and women's teams was held in February, with Spain taking the honours for the men and South Africa for the women. The competitions for both men and women was split into two groups with the top two teams after the preliminary rounds progressing through to the semi-finals.

The following is a list of international ice hockey competitions where National Hockey League players have been able to participate.

Summit Series

The Summit Series was an eight game challenge series between the Soviet National Team and a Canadian team made up of NHL hockey players. No World Hockey Association players were included in the event. Two years later, the World Hockey Association competed in the 1974 Summit Series and were defeated by the Soviets, but with no NHLers.

Year	Winner	Runner-up
1972	Canada	USSR

Super Series

The Super Series were exhibition games between Soviet teams and NHL teams that took place on each NHL opponents' home ice in North America from 1976 to 1991. The Soviet teams were usually club teams from the Soviet hockey league. The exception was in 1983, when the Soviet National Team represented the Soviet Union. Soviet teams won 14 series, NHL teams won 2 series, and 2 series were tied.

In the following summary the winner of a series is in bold.

Year	1st Team	2nd Team	W	L	T	
1976	HC CSKA	Moscow	NHL	2	1	1
1976	Soviet Wings	Moscow	NHL	3	1	0
1978	HC Spartak	Moscow	NHL	3	2	0
1979	Soviet Wings	Moscow	NHL	2	1	1
1980	HC Dynamo	Moscow	NHL	2	1	1
1980	HC CSKA	Moscow	NHL	3	2	0
1983	USSR	NHL	4	2	0	
1986	HC CSKA	Moscow	NHL	5	1	0
1986	HC Dynamo	Moscow	NHL	2	1	1
1989	HC CSKA	Moscow	NHL	4	2	1
1989	NHL	Dynamo	Riga	4	2	1
1990	NHL	Khimik	Voskresensk3		3	0
1990	NHL	SovietWingsMoscow		3	1	1
1990	HC CSKA	Moscow	NHL	4	1	0
1990	HC Dynamo	Moscow	NHL	3	2	0
1991	NHL	Khimik	Voskresensk3		3	1
1991	HC CSKA	Moscow	NHL	6	1	0
1991	HC Dynamo	Moscow	NHL	3	2	2

Canada Cup

Canada Cups were the major international competition for NHL players before the advent of the World Cup.

Year	Winner	Runner-up
1976	Canada	Czechoslovakia
1981	USSR	Canada
1984	Canada	Sweden
1987	Canada	USSR
1991	Canada	United States

Challenge Cup 1979

Year	Winner	Runner-up
1979	USSR	NHL All-Stars

Rendez Vous 1987

In 1987 two matches were held between the USSR and NHL All Stars in Quebec City, Canada in place of the annual *NHL All Star Game*. These series were considered to have no clear winner by Canadians, although the USSR scored one more goal than did the NHL All Stars.

Game	Date	Winner	Runner-up	Score
1st	February 11, 1987	NHL All-Stars	USSR	4-3
2nd	February 13, 1987	USSR	NHL All-Stars	5-3

World Cup

In 1996, the World Cup of Hockey replaced the Canada Cup.

Year	Winner	Runner-up
1996	United States	Canada
2004	Canada	Finland

Olympics

In 1998, 2002 and 2006 the NHL has had a break in the season to allow its players to participate in the Olympics.

Year	City	Gold	Silver	Bronze
1998	Nagano, Japan	Czech R.	Russia	Finland
2002	Salt Lake City,Utah	Canada	US	Russia
2006	Turin, Italy	Sweden	Finland	Czech R

World Championships

Since 1977 there has been no limit to how many NHL players countries can send to the IIHF World Championships, but the tournament is usually played during the NHL playoffs. Because of the NHL lockout starting in 2004, all NHL players were available to participate in the 2005 Men's World Ice Hockey

Championships. Many players did however not participate because they had not played for a full season, and were therefore not in "game shape".

NATIONAL HOCKEY LEAGUE

The National Hockey League (NHL) (French: *Ligue nationale de hockey (LNH)*) is a professional ice hockey league composed of 30 teams in North America. It is the premier professional ice hockey league in the world, and one of the North American major professional sports leagues. The NHL is divided into two fifteen-team conferences, each of which consists of three five-team divisions.

The league was founded in 1917 in Montreal, Quebec, Canada with four teams, and through a series of expansions, contractions and relocations, the league is now composed of 30 teams, 24 of which are based in the United States and six in Canada.

After a labour dispute that led to the cancellation of the complete 2004–05 season, the league has staged a successful comeback, including revenue and profit growth.

Because the sport originated in Canada, Canadians have historically constituted a large majority of the players in the NHL.

Over the past 25 years, the percentages of American and European players have increased because of the NHL's continued expansion into the United States, its high standard of play compared to other leagues, and the availability of highly skilled European players. Nevertheless, more than half of the league's players on the 2005–06 roster were born in Canada.

History

Total Stanley Cup Championships defunct teams not included

Team	Titles
Montreal Canadiens	24
Toronto Maple Leafs	13
Detroit Red Wings	10
Boston Bruins	5
Edmonton Oilers	5
New York Islanders	4
New York Rangers	4
Chicago Blackhawks	3
New Jersey Devils	3
Colorado Avalanche	2
Philadelphia Flyers	2
Pittsburgh Penguins	2
Anaheim Ducks	1
Calgary Flames	1
Carolina Hurricanes	1
Dallas Stars	1
Tampa Bay Lightning	1

After a series of disputes in the Canadian National Hockey Association (NHA) between Eddie Livingstone, owner of the Toronto Blue Shirts and the owners of other teams, the owners of the Montreal Canadiens, Montreal Wanderers, Ottawa Senators, and Quebec Bulldogs met at the Windsor Hotel in Montreal to talk about the NHA's future. Their discussions eventually led to the creation of the National Hockey League in 1917; the founding teams were the Canadiens, Wanderers and Senators. A Toronto franchise, because of the dispute, was given temporarily to the Toronto Arena Corp to operate, and is often referred to as the Arenas, though they operated without a nickname.

Montreal Canadiens in 1942

Even though the league struggled to stay in business during its first decade, the NHL's teams were very successful on the ice; only once, in 1925, did a team from any other league win the Stanley Cup, and by 1926 the NHL was the only league competing for the Cup.

The NHL then started a process of expansion: the Boston Bruins (the first U.S.-based NHL franchise) and Montreal Maroons entered the league in 1924–25; the New York Americans and the Pittsburgh Pirates entered in the 1925–26 season; and the New York Rangers, Chicago Black Hawks (now spelled Blackhawks), and Detroit Cougars (now known as the Red Wings) entered in the 1926–27 season, raising the number of teams in the NHL to 10.

The Great Depression and the onset of World War II, took a toll on the league, and by 1942 the NHL was reduced to six teams. These six teams (the Montreal Canadiens, Toronto Maple Leafs, Detroit Red Wings, Chicago Black Hawks, Boston Bruins, and New York Rangers) are collectively known as the Original Six, and for the next quarter-century were the only teams in the National Hockey League.

By the mid 1960s, the desire for a network television contract in the U.S., and concerns that the Western Hockey League was planning to declare itself a major league and challenge for the Stanley Cup, spurred the NHL to undertake its first expansion since the 1920s. Six new teams were added to the NHL roster in 1967, and placed in their own newly-created division. The teams were the Philadelphia Flyers, St. Louis Blues, Minnesota North Stars, Los Angeles Kings, Oakland Seals, and Pittsburgh Penguins. Three years later, the NHL added the Vancouver Canucks and Buffalo Sabres.

In 1972, the World Hockey Association (WHA) was formed, and though it never challenged for the Stanley Cup, its status as a potential rival to the NHL did not go unnoticed. In response, the NHL decided to rush its own expansion plans by adding the New York Islanders and Atlanta Flames (which soon became the Calgary Flames) in 1972 to forestall WHA franchises in newly constructed arenas in those markets, followed by the addition of the Kansas City Scouts and Washington Capitals two years later.

The two leagues fought for the rights of players and fans until the WHA folded in 1979 as part of an agreement whereby four of the remaining six WHA teams would enter the NHL as expansion teams: the Hartford Whalers (now the Carolina Hurricanes, 1997-present), Québec Nordiques (now the Colorado Avalanche, 1996-present), Edmonton Oilers, and Winnipeg Jets (now the Phoenix Coyotes, 1996-present).

After a period of stability in the 1980s, the NHL further expanded with nine new franchises in ten years. The San Jose Sharks entered in 1991; a season later the Ottawa Senators would return to the NHL along with the addition of the Tampa Bay Lightning. In 1993, the league added two additional teams, the Mighty Ducks of Anaheim and the Florida Panthers.

Next came the Nashville Predators in 1998, the Atlanta Thrashers in 1999, and then the Minnesota Wild and the Columbus Blue Jackets in 2000, bringing the total to 30 teams.

Game

Los Angeles Kings' Mike Weaver battling for the puck against Calgary Flames' Daymond Langkow, December 21, 2005

Each National Hockey League regulation game is an ice hockey game played between two teams and is 60 minutes long. The game is composed of three 20-minute periods with an intermission of 17 minutes between periods. Television timeouts are taken at the first stoppage of play after 6, 10, and 14 minutes of elapsed time unless there is a power play or the first stoppage is the result of a goal.

In these cases the timeout will occur at the first stoppage after the penalty expires or the second stoppage after the goal. At the end of the 60 minute regulation time, the team with the most goals wins the game. If a game is tied after regulation time, overtime ensues. During the regular season, overtime is a five-minute, four-player on four-player sudden-death period, in which the first team to score a goal wins the game. Until the 2005–06 season, if no team was able to score in the 5 minute overtime, the game ended in a tie.

Beginning in 2005–06, if the game is still tied at the end of overtime, the game enters a shootout. Three players for each team in turn take a penalty shot. The team with the most goals during the three round shootout wins the game. If the game is still tied after the three shootout rounds, the shootout continues, but becomes sudden death. Whichever team ultimately wins the shootout is awarded a goal in the game score and thus awarded two points in the standings. The losing team in overtime or shootout is awarded only one. Shootout goals and saves are not tracked in hockey statistics; shootout statistics are tracked separately.

Shootouts do not occur during the playoffs. In the playoffs, sudden-death 20-minute five-on-five periods are played until one team scores. While a game could theoretically continue forever, only four games have reached five overtime periods, two have reached six, and none have gone beyond six.

Teams

Devils Islanders Rangers Flyers Penguins Bruins Sabres Canadiens Senators Maple Leafs Thrashers Hurricanes Panthers Lightning Capitals Blackhawks Blue Jackets Red Wings Predators Blues Flames Avalanche Oilers Wild Canucks Ducks Stars Kings Coyotes Sharks

The National Hockey League originated in 1917 with four teams, and through a sequence of team expansions, reductions, and relocations currently consists of 30 teams, 24 of which are based in the United States and six in Canada.

The Montreal Canadiens are the most successful franchise with 24 Stanley Cup championships; in the four major North American professional sports leagues the Montreal Canadiens are only surpassed in the number of championships by the New York Yankees of Major League Baseball, who have two more.

The next most successful franchise is the Toronto Maple Leafs with 13 Stanley Cups, but they have not won a championship since 1967. The Detroit Red Wings, with ten Stanley Cups, is the most successful American franchise.

The longest streak of winning the Stanley Cup in consecutive years is five, held by the Montreal Canadiens from 1955-56 to 1959-60; the New York Islanders (1980-1983) and the Montreal Canadiens (1976-1979) have four-year championship streaks. The 1977 edition of the Montreal Canadiens, the second of four straight Stanley Cup champions, was named by ESPN as the second greatest sports team of all-time.

Of the four major leagues in the United States, the NHL is the only league to field teams that play in two countries' capital cities, Ottawa and Washington, D.C. The league also boasts more Canadian teams than all of the other major sports leagues; the NBA, MLB, and MLS have one each, all based in Toronto.

The current league organization divides the teams into two conferences. Each conference has three divisions, and each division has five teams.

The current organization has roots in the 1998–99 season where a league realignment added two divisions to bring the total number of divisions to six; the current team alignment began with the 2000–2001 season when the Minnesota Wild and the Columbus Blue Jackets joined the league as expansion teams.

Season structure

Stanley Cup, on display at the Hockey Hall of Fame, is awarded to the league champion.For more details on this topic, see Season structure of the NHL.

The National Hockey League season is divided into a regular season from the first Wednesday in October through the beginning of April, when teams play each other in a predefined schedule, and a playoffs from April to the beginning of June, which is an elimination tournament where two teams play against each other to win a best-of-seven series in order to advance to the next round. The final remaining team is crowned the Stanley Cup champion.

In the regular season, each team plays 82 games; 41 games at home and 41 on the road. Currently, of the 82 games, teams play 32 games within their division (8 games against each team in the division), 40 games against non-divisional intra-conference opponents (4 games against each team in two other divisions of the same conference) and 10 inter-conference games (1 game against each team in two of the three divisions in the opposite conference).

The two divisions from the opposite conference which each team plays against are rotated every year, much like interleague play in baseball. Points are awarded for each game, where two points are awarded for a win, one point for losing in overtime or a shootout, and zero points for a loss in regulation. Among major professional sports leagues, the NHL is the only one to award a team points for losing in overtime.

At the end of the regular season, the team that finishes with the most points in each division is crowned the division champion with the league overall leader awarded the Presidents' Trophy. The three division champions along with the five other teams in each conference with the next highest number of points, for a total of 8 teams in each conference, qualify for the playoffs.

The division winners are seeded one through three (even if a non-division winner has a higher point total), and the next five teams with the best records in the conference are seeded four through eight.

The Stanley Cup Playoffs is an elimination tournament, where two teams battle to win a best-of-seven series in order to advance to the next round. The first round of the playoffs, or conference quarterfinals, consists of the first seed playing the eighth seed, the second playing the seventh, third playing the sixth, and the fourth playing the fifth.

In the second round, or conference semifinals, the NHL re-seeds the teams, with the top remaining conference seed playing against the lowest remaining seed, and the other two remaining conference teams pairing off. In the third round, the conference finals, the two remaining teams in each conference play each other, with the conference champions proceeding to the Stanley Cup Finals.

In each round the higher-ranked team is said to be the team with the home-ice advantage. Four of the seven games are played at this team's home venue — the first and second, and, when necessary, the fifth and seventh games — with the other games played at the lower-ranked team's home venue.

Notable players

Wayne Gretzky in a New York Rangers uniform in 1997The top five point scoring forwards in the 2006-07 season were Sidney Crosby, Joe Thornton, Vincent Lecavalier, Dany Heatley, and Martin St. Louis.

The top goal scorer was Vincent Lecavalier, followed by Heatley and Teemu Selanne The top three scoring defencemen were Scott Niedermayer, Sergei Gonchar, and Sheldon Souray, and the top goaltenders (by wins) were Martin Brodeur (48), Roberto Luongo (47), Miikka Kiprusoff (40), Marc-Andre Fleury (40), and Ryan Miller (40).

In addition to Canadian and American players, who have historically composed a large majority of NHL players, the NHL draws players from all over the world. Since the 1990s when communism collapsed in Eastern Europe and the newly formed nations did not restrict the movements of players there has been a large increase in the number of European players in the NHL. European players were drafted and signed by NHL teams in an effort to bring in more skilled offensive players.

The addition of European players has changed the style of play in the NHL considerably; European style hockey has been accepted, if not embraced, in the NHL. The league also voluntarily stops its season so that its players can play in the Winter Olympics to have the players represent their own country. Currently the NHL has players from 18 different countries, with the majority still coming from Canada.

Hockey rink

National Hockey League games are played on a hockey rink which is rectangular ice rink with rounded corners and surrounded by a wall. It measures 25.91 by 60.92 metres (85 by 200 ft) in the NHL, while international standards call for a rink measuring 29–30 metres by 60–61 metres (by 95.14–98.43 ft by 196.85–200.13 ft).

The center line divides the ice in half, and is used to judge icing violations. There are two blue lines that divide the rink roughly into thirds, which divide the ice into two attacking and one neutral zone. Near the end of both ends of the rink, there is a thin red goal line spanning the width of the ice, which is used to judge goals and icing calls.

Starting in the 2005–2006 season, after testing in the American Hockey League, a trapezoidal area behind each goal net has been introduced. The goaltender can only play the puck within that area or in front of the goal line; if the goaltender plays the puck behind the goal line and not in the trapezoidal area, a 2 minute minor penalty for delay of game is assessed by the referees.

Rules

While the National Hockey League follows the general rules of ice hockey, it differs slightly from those used in international games organized by the International Ice Hockey Federation (IIHF) such as the Olympics. Infractions of the rules can lead to either the stoppage of play in the case of offside and icing calls, or a penalty call for more serious infractions.

During the 2004-05 lockout, the league changed some of the rules regarding being offside. First, the league removed the "offside pass" or "two-line pass" rule, which required a stoppage in play if a pass originating from inside a team's defending zone was completed on the offensive side of the center line, unless the puck crossed the line before the player.

Furthermore, the league reinstated the "tag-up offside" which allows an attacking player a chance to get back onside by returning to the neutral zone. The changes to the offside rule were one of several rule changes intended to increase overall scoring, which had been in decline since the expansion years of the mid-nineties.

Another rule difference between the NHL and the IIHF rules concerns how icings are called. In the NHL, a linesman stops play due to icing if a defending player (other than the goaltender) touches the puck before an attacking player is able to, in contrast to the IIHF rules where play is stopped the moment the puck crosses the goal line.

As a result of the rule changes following the 2004-05 lockout, when a team is guilty of icing the puck they are not allowed to make a line change before the following faceoff

In regards to penalties, the NHL, in addition to the minor and double minor penalties called in IIHF games, calls major penalties which are more dangerous infractions of the rules, such as fighting, and have a duration of five minutes. This is in contrast to the IIHF rule, in which players who fight are ejected from the game.

Usually a penalized team cannot replace a player that is penalized on the ice and is thus shorthanded for the duration of the penalty, but if the penalties are coincidental, such as with fighting, both teams remain at full strength.

Also, unlike minor penalties, major penalties must be served to their full completion, regardless of number of goals scored during the power play.

The NHL and the NHLPA created a stringent anti-doping policy in the new CBA in September of 2005. The policy provides for a 20-game penalty for a first positive test, 60 games for a second positive test, and a third offence resulting in a permanent ban.

Trophies and awards

The National Hockey League presents several trophies each year. The most prestigious team award is the Stanley Cup, which is awarded to the league champion at the end of the Stanley Cup playoffs. The team that has the most points in the regular season is awarded the Presidents' Trophy.

There are also numerous trophies that are awarded to players based on their statistics during the regular season; they include, among others, the Art Ross Trophy for the league scoring champion (goals and assists), the Maurice 'Rocket' Richard Trophy for the goal-scoring leader, and the William M. Jennings Trophy for the goalkeeper(s) for the team with the fewest goals against them. For the 2006–07 season these statistics-based trophies were awarded to Sidney Crosby of the Pittsburgh Penguins, Vincent Lecavalier of the Tampa Bay Lightning, and, dually, Niklas Bäckström and Manny Fernandez of the Minnesota Wild respectively.

The other player trophies are voted on by the Professional Hockey Writers Association or the team general managers. The most prestigious individual award is the Hart Memorial Trophy which is awarded annually to the Most Valuable Player; the voting is conducted by members of the Professional Hockey Writers Association to judge the player who is the most valuable to his team during the regular season. The Vezina Trophy is awarded annually to the person deemed the best goalkeeper as voted on by the general managers of the teams in the NHL. The James Norris Memorial Trophy is awarded annually to the National Hockey League's top defenceman, the Calder Memorial Trophy is awarded annually to the top rookie, and the Lady Byng Memorial Trophy is awarded to the player deemed to combine the highest degree of skill and sportsmanship; all three of these awards are voted on by members of the Professional Hockey Writers Association.

The Hockey Hall of Fame in downtown TorontoIn addition to the regular season awards, the Conn Smythe Trophy is awarded annually to the most valuable player during the NHL's Stanley Cup playoffs.

Furthermore, the top coach in the league wins the Jack Adams Award as selected by a poll of the National Hockey League Broadcasters Association. The National Hockey League publishes the names of the top three vote getters for all awards, and then names the award winner during the NHL Awards Ceremony.

Players, coaches, officials, and team builders who have had notable careers are eligible to be voted into the Hockey Hall of Fame. Players cannot enter until three years have passed since their last professional game, the shortest such time period of any major sport. One unique consequence has been Hall of Fame members (specifically, Gordie Howe, Guy Lafleur, and Mario Lemieux) coming out of retirement to play once more.

In the past, however, if a player was deemed significant enough, the pending period would be waived; only ten individuals have been honoured in this manner. In 1999, Wayne Gretzky became the last player to have the three-year restriction waived, and after Gretzky's induction, the NHL declared that he would be the last to have the waiting period omitted.

Labour Issues

There have been three league-wide work stoppages in NHL history, all happening between 1992 and 2005. The first was a strike by the National Hockey League Players Association in April 1992 which lasted for 10 days, but the strike was settled quickly and all affected games were rescheduled.

A lockout at the start of the 1994–95 season forced the league to reduce the schedule from 84 games to just 48, with the teams playing only intra-conference games during the reduced season. The resulting collective bargaining agreement was set for renegotiation in 1998 and extended to September 15, 2004.

With no new agreement in hand when the existing contract expired on September 15, 2004, league commissioner Gary Bettman announced a lockout of the players union and cessation of operations by the NHL head office. The lockout shut down the league for 310 days, the longest in sports history; the NHL was the first professional sports league to lose an entire season.

The league vowed to install what it dubbed "cost certainty" for its teams, but the NHL Players Association countered that the move was little more than a euphemism for a salary cap, which the union initially said it would not accept. A new collective bargaining agreement was ratified in July 2005 with a term of six years with an option of extending the collective bargaining agreement for an additional year at the end of the term, allowing the NHL to resume as of the 2005–06 season.

On October 5, 2005, the first post-lockout NHL season took to the ice with 15 games; and consequently all 30 teams. Of those 15 games, 11 were in front of sell-out crowds. The NHL received record attendance in the 2005–06 season. 20,854,169 fans, an average of 16,955 per game, was a 1.2% increase over the previous mark held in the 2001–02 season.

Also, the Montreal Canadiens, Colorado Avalanche, and the Vancouver Canucks sold out all of their home games; all six Canadian teams played to 98% capacity or better at every home game. 24 of the 30 clubs finished even or ahead of their 2003–04 mark. The Pittsburgh Penguins had the highest increase at 33%, mainly because of 18-year-old first overall draft pick Sidney Crosby.

Popularity

The NHL is considered one of the four major professional sports leagues in the USA, along with Major League Baseball, the National Football League, and the National Basketball Association. Hockey has the smallest total fan base of the four leagues, the smallest revenue from television, and the least sponsorship.

In contrast, hockey is the most popular of these four major sports in Canada. The NHL fan base is also the most affluent and well educated of the four. Thus, NHL season ticket prices have traditionally been higher (given the number of games per season) than the other sports.

Television and radio

In Canada, National Hockey League games are aired nationally by the Canadian Broadcasting Corporation (CBC) and The Sports Network (TSN). Regional games are broadcast by a number of networks including Rogers Sportsnet (RSN). French language games are broadcast by the Réseau des sports (RDS), but no longer is on Radio-Canada (the French-language counterpart of the CBC), which created a controversy in French-speaking Canada.

The program Hockey Night in Canada, usually aired on Saturday nights on CBC, is a long-standing Canadian tradition since first airing on television in 1952, and even prior to that on radio since the 1920s. During the playoffs, the CBC airs all games that involve Canadian teams and the Stanley Cup finals; TSN airs certain other games during the first three rounds.

In the United States NHL games are aired nationally by Versus (previously the "Outdoor Life Network" and "OLN"), and by NBC. NBC replaced the previous over-the-air network, ABC, and has a revenue-sharing agreement with the NHL.

Versus replaced ESPN as the cable network; Comcast, which owns Versus, offered a two-year $120 million agreement, while ESPN offered a revenue sharing agreement. In addition, select games are broadcast in high definition on the HDNet cable channel.

Versus has about 20 million fewer subscribers than ESPN, but Comcast switched Versus from a digital tier to basic cable to make NHL games available to more cable subscribers. For Versus the NHL coverage was a good addition as Versus' ratings grew by about 275% when it showed an NHL game, but television ratings in the United States have seen record lows.

Versus posted a 0.4 rating for the 2006 playoffs while ESPN posted a 0.7 rating two years ago; NBC posted a rating of 1.1, compared to ABC's 1.5 rating two years ago.

In Canada, for the first four games of the Stanley Cup finals, the CBC averaged 2.63 million viewers, and RDS averaged 346,000 viewers. In the United States ratings fared worse due to the inclusion of two small-market teams, including one Canadian team; the first two games on Versus posted a 0.9 rating (621,000 households), and game 3 and game 4 on NBC had ratings of 1.6 and

2.0 respectively (1.7 million and 2.2 million households). In 1994, when the New York Rangers were involved, game 7 of the Stanley Cup finals posted a rating of 5.2. Game 7 of the 2006 Stanley Cup finals gained the highest Stanley Cup rating in the series with a rating of 3.5 (3.8 million households), but it was down from the previous season's game 7 final.

XM Satellite Radio is the official satellite radio broadcaster of the NHL, as of July 1, 2007. Between September 2005 and June 2007, the NHL's broadcasting rights were shared with both XM and Sirius Satellite Radio and were broadcast on just Sirius before the NHL lockout.

Outside of North America, NHL games are broadcast across Europe on NASN (North American Sports Network) which takes feeds from Versus, FSN, TSN and CBC, including Hockey Night in Canada. Games can also be seen in the UK on Five.

Bibliography

American Sport Education Program, *Coaching Youth Hockey (Coaching Youth Series)*, Sep 2001.

Bryan Jones, *SportSpectator Field Hockey Guide: Basic Field Hockey Rules and Strategies*, Sep 2005.

Bryant Urstadt, *The Greatest Hockey Stories Ever Told: The Finest Writers on Ice (Greatest)*, Sep 1, 2006.

Claire Mitchell-Taverner, *Field Hockey Techniques & Tactics*, Nov 2, 2004.

Dave Chambers, *The Incredible Hockey Drill Book*, Sep 1, 1995

Don Macadam and Gail Reynolds, *52-Week Hockey Training (52-Week Sport Training Series)* Dec 2001.

Elizabeth Anders and Sue Myers, *Field Hockey: Steps to Success*, Jan 1999.

John Davidson and Chris McDonell, *For the Love of Hockey: Hockey Stars' Personal Stories*, Sep 14, 2007.

John Davidson and John Steinbreder, *Hockey for Dummies*, Sep 28, 2000.

Katrin Barth and Lutz Nordmann, *Learning Field Hockey*, Mar 30, 2007.

Kimberly Jo Simac, *When I Grow Up I'm Going to Be a Hockey Star*, Jan 2005.

Matt Napier, *Z Is For Zamboni: A Hockey Alphabet Edition 1. (Sleeping Bear Press Sports)* Nov 17, 2002

Michael A. Smith, *Hockey Drill Book*, Sep 1, 1996.

Michael A. Smith, *The Hockey Play Book: Teaching Hockey Systems*, Aug 6, 2005.

Michael Mckinley, *Hockey: A People's History*, Sep 19, 2006

Michael Mckinley, *Hockey: A People's History*, Sep 19, 2006.

P. J. Harari and Dave Ominsky, *Ice Hockey Made Simple: A Spectator's Guide (4th Edition)* (Spectator Guide Series), Sep 1, 2002.

Peter Maloney and Felicia Zekauskas, *The Magic Hockey Stick (Picture Puffins)* Oct 1, 2001.

Peter Twist, *Complete Conditioning for Hockey*, Jan 8, 2007.

Robert G. Price, *Ultimate Guide to Weight Training for Hockey (Ultimate Guide to Weight Training for Hockey) (Ultimate Guide to Weight Training for Hockey)* Oct 1, 2005.

Roch Carrier, Sheldon Cohen, and Sheila Fischman, *The Hockey Sweater*, Sep 1, 1985.

Roger Bradfield, *The Flying Hockey Stick*, Feb 2007.

Saul L. Miller, *Hockey Tough*, August 2003.

Stan and Shirley Fischler, *Everybody's Hockey Book*, 1983.

Index